RETIREMENT BLUEPRINT:

FINDING YOUR 210 LIFE

PHIL COOPER | 210 FINANCIAL

Phil Cooper/210 Financial
100 B Yordy Rd, Morton, Illinois 61550
www.210financial.com

Book layout ©2023 Advisors Excel, LLC

210 RETIREMENT/PHIL COOPER

ISBN 9798373284851

"Everyone to whom much was given,
of him much will be required."

~ Luke 12:48

*This book is dedicated
to those that live the 210 Life every day.*

*To my mom, my greatest inspiration. Through pain she
displayed grace and brought color to this world. A friend of
everyone and life to me.
Love you, Mom*

To my wife Kelly, the one that makes my life worth living.

*To my kids, Kendall, Carrie, Katie, and Mac:
You guys are the reason why Mom and I get out of bed
every day.*

*To my grandsons, Ky and Cash:
The joy in my heart and the smile on my face.*

I love you with a 210 heart.

Table of Contents

The 210 Life: What Is It? And Why Seek It? i

Longevity.. 9

Taxes 31

Market Volatility.. 37

Retirement Income 43

Social Security.. 59

401(k)s & IRAs 73

Annuities... 85

Estate & Legacy 93

Women Retire Too 103

Charity... 115

Finding a Financial Professional........................... 123

About the Author... 129

The 210 Life:
What Is It? And Why Seek It?

My childhood included great trials, the kind of trials that had the potential to destroy a life or at least limit the chances for anything but pain and poverty. I was raised in a home that was in constant chaos. We constantly moved, mostly when the rent was due. My parents always looked for another rental house where someone would give us another chance to prove that we would try and pay the payment.

However, there was no money, no peace, and certainly no family unity. Alcohol and its ugly darkness permeated our home and impacted everyone. My parents were blue-collar, hard-working people, but they seemed to have given up ever accomplishing their dreams. Instead, they relinquished those dreams to the numbing effects of alcohol by trying to drown their pain and all the possibility of raising five kids.

Watching this transpire proved difficult, though living with all the disharmony became even more problematic. I remember my mom telling me that she dreamed of being a veterinarian, and my dad always wanted to own land and have a small farm. Instead, they worked paycheck to paycheck and lived from bottle to bottle just trying to survive and cope with the stress of life. We grew up in a small town, where everyone knows your name and, unfortunately, know mostly every detail of your life.

It became hard to hide the fact that my family wasn't exactly the poster-family that everyone dreams of.

In those moments, I can remember saying to myself that I would not live my life this way. It wasn't like I had a lightning bolt moment of decision, but instead, it was a thousand little decisions over and over throughout my childhood that prompted me to tell myself, "Not me, I am going to win." I could not stand to watch the pain of poverty that I saw in my mom's eyes or the pain of trying to provide for a family that took my dad down into a life of despair. There had to be a better way. I looked around at my friends, and their families seemed to have figured it out, why not us?

It wasn't until late into my teens that I finally learned that it wasn't some magic formula that others discovered or some kind of privilege I did not enjoy. No, my family was on a different path, racked with pain and worries, because of decisions made over and over in the minds and hearts of my parents. They had chosen this lifestyle, oh maybe not consciously, but they chose this way of life by making decisions that had compounded over time, to only wake up one day in a place where their dreams had vanished, and hopelessness had set in.

I was in my junior year of high school when I met a cute blonde girl working in the school library. To a young boy, she was mesmerizing. I had to find a way to ask her out. I worked up the courage (through much coercing from my buddies) and finally asked her on a date. She said yes, and like they say, the rest is history. We dated all through high school and then married and began our own life: the quintessential high school sweetheart story. Kelly is her name; she has now been my wife for over thirty years. We raised three wonderful children together, and we have made a life that would only look foreign to the boy that I described earlier.

This is where 210 happened; this is where my life began; this is the reason for this book. Kelly knew all about my childhood and my family. She and I decided that we would not live a life like that. Instead, we would chase our dreams, break generational chains of financial bondage, and raise a family that had a legacy they could be proud of.

We started on this journey, and the primary non-negotiable decision we made was that we were going to buy just one home in our life, and we were going to raise our kids in that home and give them a place of stability, peace, and love. This stability would be a stark contrast to my upbringing of moving every time the rent was due and never being able to look back to a place that I could remember was "home." I wanted to give my kids a place they could always call home, no matter where they were in this world or what was going on in their lives. They could always point their compass home—to a place full of love and peace, and a place where mom and dad would be together. We did just that. We bought a home and made a life exactly as I described. The address of the home that we bought starts with 210. Our home is 210 and that is where 210 Financial was born.

Thank you for letting me share my background and why we named our financial advisory company 210 Financial. One harrowing experience involving one of my daughters reveals just how dangerous things when precautions get taken for granted.

****

Dad, we have a problem! Those are the words that I heard on the other end of the phone at 2 o'clock in the morning. My eighteen-year-old daughter had been driving her car when a tire came off. She made a call no parent wants to field in the middle of the night and began telling me of the mishap.

As any dad would do, I jumped out of bed and drove as fast as I could to where she got stranded. My mind raced uncontrollably knowing she pulled over on the side of the road and needing to make sure she was okay.

Thankfully, I found her and drove her home safe and sound.

Just that morning I had new tires put on her car. The technician failed to tighten the lug nuts and the tire literally came off the car. This could have turned out much worse than it did. Thankfully, the outcome is nothing more than a funny story told by a father who still thinks about the disastrous way his daughter's car breakdown could have gone.

So what is my point? Why am I telling you this?

Because just a tiny detail and some attention to excellence would have allowed my daughter to drive safely. Instead, someone did a sloppy job putting new tires on her vehicle and called it good, placing a teenage girl in danger and potentially changing her life.

I see this every day in the lives of people that have made sloppy and careless mistakes with financial matters. They have done a few things and called it good, only to get down the road of retirement and then have a tire come off and jeopardize their financial wherewithal.

Many potential risks can be reduced with a well-thought-out, well-crafted financial plan. The tires of your financial plan can stay tight and balanced, helping maintain the retirement vision you have always wanted.

One of the major considerations in the construction of your plan needs to be expenses. There is an adage that says "your outgo cannot exceed your income or it will be your upkeep that is your downfall." In other words, you have to account for your expenses and you have to plan for them to be less than your income. It seems simple, but it also seems so many people do not have a handle on this part of their life. This is a crucial element to your financial future. Creating a budget and living within that budget can provide you real financial freedom—the kind of freedom that you have looked forward to for many years.

A professional planner can help you create a plan and then hold you accountable to that plan, greatly increasing your chance for success.

At 210 Financial, we take a fresh approach to planning your future. We start with the end in mind. We look down the road at your goals and dreams, then we craft a plan designed to help get you there. We call our planning process the "retirement blueprint." Any good construction job requires a good blueprint to work from. That is what we do, we build the blueprint plans then we help you construct the foundation, floor, walls, and ultimately the roof for your financial future.

Over the last few decades, we have helped many people plan to live out out a full and rewarding life. What a joy to be a part of these dear dreams, and to watch families manage their lives in ways that fulfill their legacy—taking those trips, paying for college, and experiencing once-in-a-lifetime goals. We've watched with delight as grandpas coach little league, grandmas become room mothers, and parents teach their kids how to save and prosper. This is what life is all about, doing it the way that you have always dreamed of. This is possible for you too! It takes a plan, but the good news is that a plan is available to you! That is what we do at 210 Financial. We build plans but more importantly, we build upon dreams!

Potential Risks to Your Ideal Retirement

Ever feel like life gets in the way and prevents you from doing things you should not ignore? I think if we're honest with ourselves, we've all put off obligations we know are important.

In your case, you may be reading this book because it's time to get serious about financial planning and, specifically, devising a way to best prepare for retirement. A retirement plan should be based on more components than just your investments or your finances. The preparation of that strategy begins with your desires, ambitions, and goals for this fulfilling season of life.

There's no such thing as a silly question. Not when one of the most common questions we hear from folks regarding retirement is, "Am I going to be okay?" Often, it seems, people are reluctant to meet with financial professionals because they worry they might sound uneducated. Yet, it's understandable for you to be a novice when it comes to financial issues and retirement concerns. You've been busy with your lives and your careers. Time spent away from work has meant time spent being around those you love and engaging in the activities you enjoy. Retirement provides the opportunity to do even more of that, while not fretting over work obligations.

Concerns people have about what they may encounter during retirement can be far-reaching and still perfectly legitimate. For a quick snapshot, I want to provide a brief sampling of wide-ranging issues that can come up during discussions about what to potentially brace for in retirement. This book will touch on many of these issues in further detail.

Politics: A presidential election often stirs emotions regarding potential effects on the economy. Investors grow anxious about how a new president can influence market returns. It's Congress, however, that establishes tax laws and passes spending bills. Yet the president can indirectly affect the economy and the stock market in various ways such as the appointment of policymakers, development of international relations, and influential sway on new legislation.

Taxes: An example of a president's influence can be cited in signature legislation passed during Donald Trump's presidency, the Tax Cuts and Jobs Act of 2017. However, our tax system remains progressive, so the more you earn, the higher the tax rate within each tax bracket of subsequently higher income. A thorough understanding of tax regulations can be crucial. A financial professional can help identify potential issues a tax professional can help solve.

Inflation: Government spending, which most recently spiked with relief packages designed to assist U.S. citizens during the COVID-19 pandemic, can fuel concerns of inflationary hikes stemming from an influx of money thrust at the same consumer goods. A retiree's income can be jeopardized by the effect inflation can have on a fixed budget. The value of currency decreases because inflation erodes purchasing power.

Health pandemic: The coronavirus outbreak could impact how Americans view risks and re-examine healthy habits. That, potentially, could be one of the effects of COVID-19 as we assess how long a pandemic can last and if others will occur in our lifetimes. The cost of health care can be surprising throughout retirement. It could become an issue people focus on even more following the pandemic, which had a particularly acute impact on some U.S. elder care facilities.

Cybersecurity: Think you'll give up your smartphone in retirement? No way, right? It's here to stay, along with other intellectual gadgetry, including devices that have not been patented or invented. Retirees are becoming more tech-savvy, yet they can also be more trusting, which can be problematic when responding to potential scammers by phone, text, or email. Cybercrime often uses technology to target potential victims. Scammers, much like technology, figure to only grow more sophisticated over time.

CHAPTER 1

Longevity

Y ou would think the prospect of the grave would loom more frightening as we age, yet many retirees say their number one concern is actually running out of money in their twilight years.[1] This fear is, unfortunately, justified, in part, because of one significant factor: We're living longer.

According to the Social Security Administration, in 1950, the average life expectancy for a sixty-five-year-old man was seventy-eight, and the average for a sixty-five-year-old woman was eighty-one. In 2021, those averages were eighty-three and eighty-eight, respectively.[2]

The bottom line of many retirees' budget woes comes down to this: They just didn't plan to live so long. Now, when we are younger and in our working years, that's not something we necessarily see as a bad thing; don't some people fantasize about living forever or, at least, reaching the ripe old age of one hundred?

However, with a longer lifespan, as we near retirement, we face a few snags. Our resources are finite—we only have so much money to provide income—but our lifespans can be

---

[1] Liz Weston. nerdwallet.com. March 25, 2021. "Will You Really Run Out of Money in Retirement?"
https://www.nerdwallet.com/article/finance/will-you-really-run-out-of-money-in-retirement
[2] Social Security Administration. 2011 Trustees Report. "Actuarial Publications: Cohort Life Expectancy."
https://www.ssa.gov/OACT/TR/2011/lr5a4.html

unpredictably long, perhaps longer than our resources allow. Also, longer lives don't necessarily equate with healthier lives. The longer you live, the more money you will likely need to spend on health care, even excluding long-term care needs like nursing homes.

You will also run into inflation. If you don't plan to live another twenty-five years but end up doing so, inflation at an average 3 percent will approximately double the price of goods over that time period. Put a harsh twist on that and the buying power of a ninety-year-old will be half of what they possessed if they retired at sixty-five.[3]

Because we don't necessarily get to have our cake and eat it, too, our collective increased longevity hasn't necessarily increased the healthy years of our lives. Typically, our life-extending care most widely applies to the time in our lives where we will need more care in general. Think of common situations like a pacemaker at eighty-five, or cancer treatment at seventy-eight.

"Wow, Phil," I can hear you say. "Way to start with the good news first."

I know, I've painted a grim picture, but all I'm concerned about here is cost. It's hard to put a dollar sign on life, but that is essentially what we're talking about when discussing longevity and finances. According to the Stanford Center on Longevity, more than half of pre-retirees underestimate the life expectancy of the average sixty-five-year-old.[4] Living longer isn't a bad thing; it just costs more, and one key to a sound retirement strategy is preparing for it in advance.

I want to share a story about a wonderful couple, Bill and Mary. Although these are not their real names, their outcome is consistent with those who have followed a financial plan.

---

[3] Bob Sullivan, Benjamin Curry. Forbes. April 28, 2021. "Inflation And Retirement Investments: What You Need to Know." https://www.forbes.com/advisor/retirement/inflation-retirement-investments/

[4] Stanford Center on Longevity. "Underestimating Years in Retirement." http://longevity.stanford.edu/underestimating-years-in-retirement/

Bill and Mary were nearing retirement and decided that they needed the advice of a professional to "make sure" they were on the right path toward a successful financial future. They made a call to our office and met with our team. They were so excited to be this close to realizing their dreams of travel, time spent with grandkids, and just not having to wake up on Monday morning and run the rat race. They had done a good job of accumulating funds in their 401(k)s and were debt-free. All indications were they were going to be "okay." However, they had no plan if something happened and one of them passed away prematurely.

Bill had retired from a company with a pension but Mary had chosen to stay at home and raise kids, leaving her without a pension. We asked Bill what happens to his pension if he were to pass away. He told us that it disappears completely, leaving Mary with no income at all except Social Security. Bill's plan was to have Mary live off of the proceeds from their 401(k)s. The problem is that due to the amount of monthly income that they needed, if Bill died, Mary would have likely run out of money at about age eighty-two.

Is this a problem? Not if Mary dies before that. But what if she lives longer? We showed this to Bill and his heart sunk. He had no idea of the risk they took on. However, it was possible to look into solutions that could provide an income stream Mary could never outlive.

Addressing the financial hardships a surviving spouse could incur is a crucial step in building a suitable financial plan. It is one of the first considerations we examine when constructing a retirement income plan. Such plans are not solvent if the death of a spouse causes a significant reduction in funds needed to maintaining the livelihood of a survivor.

Living longer may be more expensive, but it can be so meaningful when you plan for your "just-in-cases."

Retiring Early

A key part of planning for retirement revolves around retirement income. After all, retirement is cutting the cord that tethers you to your employer—and your monthly check. However, that check often comes with many other benefits, particularly health care. Health care is often the thing that can unexpectedly put dreams for an early retirement on hold. Some employers offer health benefits to their retired workers, but that number has declined drastically over the past several decades. In 1988, among employers who offered health benefits to their workers, 66 percent offered health benefits to their retirees. That number has since diminished to 29 percent.[5]

So, with employer-offered retirement health benefits on the wane, this becomes a major point of concern for anyone who is looking to retire, particularly those who are looking to retire before age sixty-five, when they would become eligible for Medicare coverage. Fidelity estimates that the average retired couple at age sixty-five will need approximately $315,000 for medical expenses, not including long-term care.[6] Do you think it's likely that cost will decrease?

Even if you are working until age sixty-five or have plans to cover your health expenses until that point, I often have clients who incorrectly assume Medicare is their golden ticket to cover all expenses. That is simply not the case.

---

[5] Henry J. Kaiser Family Foundation. October 8, 2020. "2020 Employer Health Benefits Survey Section Eleven: Retiree Health Benefits." https://www.kff.org/report-section/ehbs-2020-section-11-retiree-health-benefits/

[6] Fidelity Viewpoints. Fidelity. August 29, 2022. "How to Plan for Rising Health Care Costs." https://www.fidelity.com/viewpoints/personal-finance/plan-for-rising-health-care-costs

Retiring Later

Planning for a long life in retirement partly depends on when you retire. While many people end up retiring earlier than they anticipated—due to injuries, layoffs, family crises, and other unforeseen circumstances—continuing to work past age sixty (and even sixty-five) is still a viable option for others and can be an excellent way to help establish financial comfort in retirement.

There are many reasons for this. For one, you obviously still earn a paycheck and the benefits accompanying it. Medical coverage and beefing up your retirement accounts with further savings can be significant by themselves but continuing your income also should keep you from dipping into your retirement funds, further allowing them the opportunity to grow.

Additionally, for many workers, their nine-to-five job is more than just clocking in and out. Having a sense of purpose can keep us active physically, mentally, and socially. That kind of activity and level of engagement may also help stave off many of the health problems that plague retirees. Avoiding a sedentary life is one of the advantages of staying plugged into the workforce, if possible.

How long should a person work? When should a person retire? The answers are specific to the goals and dreams of each person.

A few thought starters:

1. Do I like what I am doing at work?
2. Is the work fulfilling to me?
3. Would I rather be doing something else?
4. Is my job draining my energy and disrupting my peace?
5. How will I draw income if my paycheck stops?

Retirement is so much more than age or financial ability. I believe that each of us has a calling to fulfill, and for some, that calling is a career. However, for some, work is drudgery. If that is you, then start by asking yourself what it is that really makes you happy, content, and fulfilled.. Retirement could indeed be an option. The creation of a financial plan allows you to have choices. You may decide that another job is better for you, or you may be fulfilled by volunteering your time to a cause near and dear to your heart.

Either way, you need a plan.

Let's look at two examples:

First, we have Linda. She decided to retire early and just relax. Financially, she was well off and had no need for the income that her job supplied. Within a very short period of time, she grew bored and depressed. She found out that her job was giving her much more than income; it also provided a sense of purpose. Linda decided to volunteer her time to a local ministry and she once again found purpose in her life. Just as importantly, a young person that needed the money took her old job and had a good income for their family. The situation became a win-win proposition.

Now let's look at Barb, She decided to retire early for many of the same reasons as Linda. However, Barb had a different idea. She was planning on travel and time spent with family as a way to fulfill her time. It worked! She retired and has never been happier. She travels the world taking her kids and grandkids on dream vacations. She wakes up every day with a new sense of adventure. Barb spent time creating a great financial plan that gave her income, reduced investment risk, and provide the confidence she needed to take the plunge and leave the workforce.

So what is the point? The point is that no matter your reasons for wanting to retire or wanting to work, you need a financial plan that looks out for your financial well-being and includes funds that help provide a purpose for your life. We help each of our clients think through this transitionary period so that they are better equipped for retirement's financial and emotional aspects.

Health Care

Take a second to reflect on your health care plan. Although working up to or even past age sixty-five would allow you to avoid a coverage gap between your working years and Medicare, that may not be an option for you. Even if it is, when you retire, you will need to make some decisions about what kind of insurance coverage you may need to supplement your Medicare. Are there any medical needs you have that may require coverage in addition to Medicare? Did your parents or grandparents have any inherited medical conditions you might consider using a special savings plan to cover?

These are all questions that are important to review with your financial professional so you can be sure you have enough money put aside for health care.

Long-Term Care

Longevity means the need for long-term care is statistically more likely to happen. If you intend to pass on a legacy, planning for long-term care is paramount, since most estimates project nearly 70 percent of Americans will need some type of it.[7] However, this may be one of the biggest, most stressful pieces of longevity planning I encounter in my work. For one thing, who wants to talk about the point in their lives when they may feel the most limited? Who wants to dwell on what will happen if they no longer can toilet, bathe, dress, or feed themselves?

I get it; this is a less-than-fun part of planning. But a little bit of preparation now can go a long way!

When it comes to your longevity, just like with your goals, one of the important things to do is sit and dream. It may not be the fun, road-trip-to-the-Grand-Canyon kind of dreaming,

---

[7] LongTermCare.gov. February 18, 2020. "How Much Care Will You Need?" https://acl.gov/ltc/basic-needs/how-much-care-will-you-need

but you can spend time envisioning how you want your twilight years to look.

For instance, if it is important for you to live in your home for as long as possible, who will provide for the day-to-day fixes and to-dos of housework if you become ill? Will you set aside money for a service, or do you have relatives or friends nearby whom you could comfortably allow to help you? Do you prefer in-home care over a nursing home or assisted living? This could be a good time to discuss the possibility of moving into a retirement community versus staying where you are or whether it's worth moving to another state and leaving relatives behind.

These are all important factors to discuss with your spouse and children, as *now* is the right time to address questions and concerns. For instance, is aging in place more important to one spouse than the other? Are the friends or relatives who live nearby emotionally, physically, and financially capable of helping you for a time if you face an illness?

Many families I meet with find these conversations very uncomfortable, particularly when children discuss nursing home care with their parents. A knee-jerk reaction for many is to promise they will care for their aging parents. This is noble and well-intentioned, but there needs to be an element of realism here. Does "help" from an adult child mean they stop by and help you with laundry, cooking, home maintenance, and bills? Or does it mean they move you into their spare room when you have hip surgery? Are they prepared to help you use the restroom and bathe if that becomes difficult for you to do on your own?

I don't mean to discourage families from caring for their own; this can be a profoundly admirable relationship when it works out. However, I've seen families put off planning for late-in-life care based on a tenuous promise that the adult children would care for their parents, only to watch as the support system crumbles. Sometimes this is because the assumed caregiver hasn't given serious thought to the preparation they would need, both in a formal sense and regarding their personal physical, emotional, and financial commitments. This is often also because we can't see the future: Alzheimer's disease and other maladies of old age can exact a heavy toll. When a loved one reaches the point where he or she is at risk of wandering away or needs help with two or more activities of daily living, it can be more than one person or family can realistically handle.

If you know what you want, communicate with your family about both the best-case and worst-case scenarios. Then, hope for the best, and plan for the worst.

Realistic Cost of Care

Wrapped up in your planning should be a consideration for the cost of long-term care. One study estimates that by 2030, the nation's long-term care costs could reach $2.5 trillion as roughly 24 million Americans require some type of long-term care.[8] The potential costs for such care and treatment can be underestimated, especially by those who have maintained robust health and find it difficult to envision future declines to their condition.

Another piece of planning for long-term care costs is anticipating inflation. It's common knowledge that prices have been and keep rising, which can lower your purchasing power on everything from food to medical care. Long-term care is a big piece of the inflation-disparity pie.

While local costs vary from state to state, here's the national median for various forms of long-term care (plus projections that account for a 3 percent annual inflation, so you can see what I am referencing):[9]

---

[8] Tara O'Neill Hayes, Sara Kurtovic. Americanactionforum.org. February 18, 2020. "The Ballooning Costs of Long-Term Care." https://www.americanactionforum.org/research/the-ballooning-costs-of-long-term-care/

[9] Genworth Financial. January 2022. "Cost of Care Survey 2021." https://www.genworth.com/aging-and-you/finances/cost-of-care.html

Long-Term Care Costs: Inflation				
	Home Health Care, Homemaker Services	Adult Day Care	Assisted Living	Nursing Home (semi-private room)
Annual 2021	$59,488	$20,280	$54,000	$94,900
Annual 2031	$79,947	$27,255	$72,571	$127,538
Annual 2041	$107,442	$36,628	$97,530	$171,400
Annual 2051	$144,393	$49,225	$131,072	$230,347

Fund Your Long-Term Care

One critical mistake I see are those who haven't planned for long-term care because they assume the government will provide everything. But that's a big misconception. The government has two health insurance programs: Medicare and Medicaid. These can greatly assist you in your health care needs in retirement but usually don't provide enough coverage to cover all your health care costs in retirement. My firm isn't a government outpost, so we don't get to make decisions when it comes to forming policy and specifics about either one of these programs. I'm going to give the overview of both, but if you want to dive into the details of these programs, you can visit www.Medicare.gov and www.Medicaid.gov.

Medicare
Medicare covers those aged sixty-five and older and those who are disabled. Medicare's coverage of any nursing-home-related

health issues is limited. It might cover your nursing home stay if it is not a "custodial" stay, and it isn't long-term. For example, if you break a bone or suffer a stroke, stay in a nursing home for rehabilitative care, and then return home, Medicare may cover you. But, if you have developed dementia or are looking to move to a nursing facility because you can no longer bathe, dress, toilet, feed yourself, or take care of your hygiene, etc., then Medicare is not going to pay for your nursing home costs.[10]

You can enroll in Medicare anytime during the three months before and four months after your sixty-fifth birthday. Miss your enrollment deadline, and you could risk paying increased premiums for the rest of your life. On top of prompt enrollment, there are a few other things to think about when it comes to Medicare, not least among them being the need to understand the different "parts," what they do, and what they don't cover.

Part A

Medicare Part A is what you might think of as "classic" Medicare. Hospital care, some types of home health care, and major medical care fall under this. While most enrollees pay nothing for this service (as they likely paid into the system for at least ten years), you may end up paying, either based on work history or delayed signup. In 2022, the highest premium was $499 per month, and a hospital stay does have a deductible, $1,556.[11] And, if you have a hospital stay that surpasses sixty days, you could be looking at additional costs; keep in mind, Medicare doesn't pay for long-term care and services.

---

[10] Medicare.gov. "What Part A covers." https://www.medicare.gov/what-medicare-covers/part-a/what-part-a-covers.html
[11] Medicare. "Medicare 2022 Costs at a Glance." https://www.medicare.gov/your-medicare-costs/medicare-costs-at-a-glance

Part B

Medicare Part B is an essential piece of wrap-around coverage for Medicare Part A. It helps pay for doctor visits and outpatient services. This also comes with a price tag: Although the Part B deductible is only $226 in 2023, you will still pay 20 percent of all costs after that, with no limit on out-of-pocket expenses. The Part B monthly premium for 2023 ranges from the standard amount of $164.90 to $560.50.[12]

Part C

Medicare Part C, more commonly known as Medicare Advantage plans, are an alternative to a combination of Parts A, B, and sometimes D. Administered through private insurance companies, these have a variety of costs and restrictions, and they are subject to the specific policies and rules of the issuing carrier.

Part D

Medicare Part D is also through a private insurer and is supplemental to Parts A and B, as its primary purpose is to cover prescription drugs. Like any private insurance plan, Part D has its quirks and rules that vary from insurer to insurer.

The Donut Hole

Even with a "Part D" in place, you may still have a coverage gap between what your Part D private drug insurance pays for your prescription and what basic Medicare pays. In 2023, the coverage gap is $4,660, meaning, after you meet your private prescription insurance limit, you will spend no more than 25

---

[12] Ibid.

percent of your drug costs out-of-pocket before Medicare will kick in to pay for more prescription drugs.[13]

Medicare Supplements

Medicare Supplement Insurance, MedSup, Medigap, or plans labeled Medicare Part F, G, H, I, J . . . Known by a variety of monikers, this is just a fancy way of saying "medical coverage for those over sixty-five that picks up the tab for whatever the federal Medicare program(s) doesn't." Again, costs, limitations, etc., vary by carrier.

Does that sound like a bunch of government alphabet soup to you? It certainly does to me. And, did you read the fine print? Unpredictable costs, varied restrictions, difficult-to-compare benefits, donut holes, and coverage gaps. That's par for the course with health care plans through the course of our adult lives. What gives? I thought Medicare was supposed to be easier, comprehensive, and at no cost!

The truth is there is probably no stage of life when health care is easy to understand.

I do not think it is a hard argument to make, and I believe that we can all agree, that health care costs are much higher than any of us ever anticipated. On average in the United State, spending on health care averaged $11,945 per person in 2020, showing that our citizens spend a greater amount on health care than those in most advanced countries.[14] This level of spending can create a significant hardship for some American families.

---

[13] Medicare. "Costs in the coverage gap."
https://www.medicare.gov/drug-coverage-part-d/costs-for-medicare-drug-coverage/costs-in-the-coverage-gap
[14] Emma Wager, Jared Ortaliza and Cynthia Cox. Peterson KFF Health System Tracker. January 21, 2022."How does health spending in the U.S. compare to other countries?" https://www.healthsystemtracker.org/chart-collection/health-spending-u-s-compare-countries-2/#GDP%20per%20capita%20and%20health%20consumption%20spending%20per%20capita,%202020%20(U.S.%20dollars,%20PPP%20adjusted)

Secondly, how about the complexity and confusion of Medicare? This trend will likely continue as the American population ages and the demand for more care increases.

Take a look around and notice the number of long-term care facilities in operation or under construction. They seem to be going up on every corner. Why? We are living much longer lives, therefore needing more and more medical care. I believe this could be one of your single greatest costs throughout retirement. This is one that can derail your finances as quickly as any other concern.

If you take nothing else from this book, consider this one topic and examine solutions for potential long-term care needs. Meet with a financial professional to help ensure your current and future health care costs are addressed and planned. Statistics are proving more and more that you are going to live longer than the previous generation, and you will most likely need more care than you thought.

Do not let this one slide! Get a plan!

The best thing you can do for yourself is to scope out the health care field early, compare costs often, and prepare for out-of-pocket costs well in advance—decades, if possible.

Medicaid

Medicaid is a program the states administer, so funding, protocol, and limitations vary. Compared to Medicare, Medicaid more widely covers nursing home care, but it targets a different demographic: those with low incomes.

If you have more assets than the Medicaid limit in your state and need nursing home care, you will need to use those assets to pay for your care. You will also have a list of additional state-approved ways to spend some of these assets over the Medicaid limit, such as pre-purchasing burial plots and funeral expenses or paying off debts. After that, your remaining assets fund your nursing home stay until they are gone, at which point Medicaid will jump in.

Some people aren't stymied by this, thinking they will just pass on their financial assets early, gifting them to relatives, friends, and causes so they can qualify for Medicaid when they need it. However, to prevent this exact scenario, Uncle Sam has implemented the look-back period. Currently, if you enroll in Medicaid, you are subject to having the government scrutinize the last five years of your finances for large gifts or expenses that may subject you to penalties, temporarily making you ineligible for Medicaid coverage.

So, if you're planning to preserve your money for future generations and retain control of your financial resources during your lifetime, you'll probably want to prepare for the costs of longevity beyond a "government plan."

Self-Funding

One way to fund a longer life is the old-fashioned way, through self-funding. There are a variety of financial tools you can use, and they all have their pros and cons. If your assets are in low-interest financial vehicles (savings, bonds, CDs), you risk letting inflation erode the value of your dollar. Or, if you are relying on the stock market, you have more growth potential, but you'll also want to consider the possible implications of market volatility. What if your assets take a hit? If you suffer a loss in your retirement portfolio in early or mid-retirement, you might have the option to "tighten your belt," so to speak, and cut back on discretionary spending to allow your portfolio the room to bounce back. But, if you are retired and depend on income from a stock account that just hit a downward stride, what are you going to do?

HSAs

These days, you might also be able to self-fund through a health savings account, or HSA, if you have access to one through a high-deductible health plan (you will not qualify to save in an HSA after enrolling in Medicare). In an HSA, any growth of your tax-deductible contributions will be tax-free, and any distributions paid out for qualified health costs are also tax-free. Long-term care expenses count as health costs, so, if this is an option available to you, it is one way to use the tax advantages to self-fund your longevity. Bear in mind, if you are younger than sixty-five, any money you use for nonqualified expenses will be subject to taxes and penalties, and, if you are older than sixty-five, any HSA money you use for non-medical expenses is subject to income tax.

LTCI

One slightly more nuanced way to pay for longevity, specifically for long-term care, is long-term care insurance, or LTCI. As car insurance protects your assets in case of a car accident and home insurance protects your assets in case something happens to your house, long-term care insurance aims to protect your assets in case you need long-term care in an at-home or nursing home situation.

As with other types of insurance, you will pay a monthly or annual premium in exchange for an insurance company paying for long-term care down the road. Typically, policies cover two to three years of care, which is adequate for an "average" situation: it's estimated 70 percent of Americans will need about three years of long-term care of some kind.

Now, there are a few oft-cited components of LTCI that make it unattractive for some:

- Expense — LTCI can be expensive. It is generally less expensive the younger you are, but a sixty-five-year-old couple who purchased LTCI in 2022 could expect to pay a combined amount of $3,750 each year for an average three-year coverage policy. And the annual cost only increases from there the older you are.[15]

- Limited options — Let's face it: LTCI may be expensive for consumers, but it can also be expensive for companies that offer it. With fewer companies willing to

---

[15] American Association for Long-Term Care Insurance. 2023. . "Long-Term Care Insurance Facts – Data – Statistics – 2022 Reports" https://www.aaltci.org/long-term-care-insurance/learning-center/ltcfacts-2022.php#2022costs-65
d

take on that expense, this narrows the market, meaning opportunities to price shop for policies with different options or custom benefits are limited.

- If you know you need it, you might not be able to get it — Insurance companies offering LTCI are taking on a risk that you may need LTCI. That risk is the foundation of the product—you may or may not need it. If you know you will need it because you have a dementia diagnosis or another illness for which you will need long-term care, you will likely not qualify for LTCI coverage.
- Use it or lose it—If you have LTCI and are in the minority of Americans who die having never needed long-term care, all the money you paid into your LTCI policy is gone.
- Possibly fluctuating rates—Your rate is not locked in on LTCI. Companies maintain the ability to raise or lower your premium amounts. This means some seniors face an ultimatum: Keep funding a policy at what might be a less affordable rate *or* lose coverage and let go of all the money they paid in so far.

After that, you might be thinking, "How can people possibly be interested in LTCI?" But let me repeat myself—as many as 70 percent of Americans will need long-term care. And, although only one in ten Americans have age fifty-five-plus purchased LTCI, keep in mind the high cost of nursing home care. Can you afford $7,000 a month to put into nursing home care and still have enough left over to protect your legacy? This is a very real concern considering one set of statistics reported a two-in-three chance that a senior citizen will become physically or cognitively impaired in their lifetime.[16] So, not to sound like a broken record, but it is vitally important to have a plan in place to deal with longevity and long-term care if you intend to leave a financial legacy.

[16] payingforseniorcare.com. 2022. "Long-Term Senior Care Statistics" https://www.payingforseniorcare.com/statistics

As with every industry, change is happening rapidly with long-term care insurance. In most cases, consumers are realizing substantial benefits. The financial services industry, especially the insurance industry, is no stranger to change. With the adoption of the internet and the information age, you can get everything you need at your fingertips. The biggest problem I see is that people are overwhelmed with information and get paralyzed by the number of choices. And therefore, they sometimes do nothing at all in terms of planning. When it comes to your long-term health care concerns, doing nothing can negatively impact your financial future.

Due to changes in the industry and consumers demanding more value, there are now more options than ever before for you to have a cost-effective plan incorporating health care and long-term care. Such plans can help you reduce the risk of exhausting your assets in the future.

I have a question for you. What do life insurance companies know about everyone?   You are going to die, and they know it. If you have a life insurance policy, they know they will write a check to your beneficiaries. They have planned for this, and they have priced their policies accordingly.

However, since they know that they are on the hook for the death benefit, they are now offering you a choice on how they pay that to you. Some companies are offering you options to receive at least part of the death benefit while you are alive if you need the money for long term care, a very creative idea indeed. It is smart for the insurance company because it can disperse funds over a series of years rather than one lump sum. Have your life insurance policy reviewed to see if it offers such an option.

A few relevant statistics to keep in mind:
- The longer you live, the more likely you are to continue living; the longer you live, the more health care you will likely need to pay for.

- The average cost of a private nursing home room in the United States in 2021 was $9,034 a month.[17] But keep in mind, that is just the nursing home—it doesn't include other medical costs, let alone pleasantries, like entertainment or hobby spending.
- In 2022, Fidelity calculated that a healthy couple retiring at age sixty-five could expect to pay around $315,000 over the course of retirement to cover health and medical expenses.

I know. Whoa, there, Phil, I was hoping to have a realistic idea of health costs, not be driven over by a cement mixer!

The good news is, while we don't know these exact costs in advance, we know there *will* be costs. And you won't have to pay your total Medicare lifetime premiums in one day as a lump sum. Now that you have a good idea of health care costs in retirement, you can *plan* for them! That's the real point, here: Planning in advance can keep you from feeling nickel-and-dimed to your wits' end. Instead, having a sizeable portion of your assets earmarked for health care can allow you the freedom to choose health care networks, coverage options, and long-term care possibilities you like and that you think offer you the best in life.

Product Riders

LTCI and self-funding are not the only ways to plan for the expenses of longevity. Some companies are getting creative with their products, particularly insurance companies. One way they are retooling to meet people's needs is through optional product riders on annuities and life insurance. Elsewhere in this book, I talk about annuity basics, but here's a brief overview: Annuities are insurance contracts. You pay the

---

[17] Genworth Financial. January 31, 2022. "Genworth 2020 Cost of Care Survey." https://www.genworth.com/aging-and-you/finances/cost-of-care.html

insurance company a premium, either as a lump sum or as a series of payments over a set amount of time, in exchange for guaranteed income payments. One of the advantages of an annuity is it has access to riders, which allow you to tweak your contract for a fee, usually about 1 percent of the contract value annually. One annuity rider some companies offer is a long-term care rider. If you have an annuity with a long-term care rider and are not in need of long-term care, your contract behaves as any annuity contract would—nothing changes. Generally speaking, if you reach a point when you can't perform multiple functions of daily life on your own, you notify the insurance company, and a representative will turn on those provisions of your contract.

Like LTCI, different companies and products offer different options. Some annuity long-term care riders offer coverage of two years in a nursing home situation. Others cap expenses at two times the original annuity's value. It greatly depends. Some people prefer this option because there isn't a "use-it-or-lose-it" piece; if you die without ever having needed long-term care, you still will have had the income benefit from the base contract. Still, as with any annuities or insurance contracts, there are the usual restrictions and limitations. Withdrawing money from the contract will affect future income payments, early distributions can result in a penalty, income taxes may apply, and, because the insurance company's solvency is what guarantees your payments, it's important to do your research about the insurance company you are considering purchasing a contract from.

Understandably, a discussion on long-term care is bound to feel at least a little tedious. Yet, this is a critical piece of planning for income in retirement, particularly if you want to leave a legacy.

How critical? I can remember a call like it was yesterday. Sue, a long-term client, informed me that John, her husband of forty-eight years, was being admitted to a nursing home. She had noticed for several months that John was just not acting normal. After what seemed to be an infinite number of visits to the doctors and countless medical tests, a diagnosis of dementia came like a crushing blow from a prize fighter's right hand.

Sue naturally felt shaken, confused, and scared. Of course, the news scared her because the love of her life now needed treatment for a life-changing illness. In addition, John had always maintained that long-term care insurance seemed "too expensive." Now, the cost to care for him had been priced at nearly $8,000 per month. That's a sizable amount of money for anyone, especially John and Sue, because they lived on a relatively meager income derived from pension and Social Security benefits.

Could this have been averted? Yes, with just a little planning and forethought, John and Sue could have carved out a small amount of their nest egg and protected themselves against this type of event. The problem that most people face is they always think, "this will never happen to me." But sometimes, it does. I am quite sure that John's intention was never to put his wife in such a difficult and scary position.

What is the point? If you love someone, anyone, take care of them today by planning for your tomorrow.

Spousal Planning

Here's one thing to keep in mind no matter how you plan to save: Many of us will be planning for more than ourselves. Look back at all the stats on health events and the likelihood of long life and long-term care. If they hold true for a single individual, then the likelihood of having a costly health or long-term care event is even higher for a married couple. You'll be planning for not just one life, but two. So, when it comes to long-term care insurance, annuities, self-funding, or whatever strategy you are looking at using, be sure you are funding longevity for the both of you.

Investing involves risk, including the potential loss of principal. No investment strategy can guarantee a profit or protect against loss in periods of declining values. Any references to protection benefits or guaranteed/lifetime income streams refer only to fixed insurance products, not securities or investment products. Insurance and annuity product guarantees are backed by the financial strength and claims-paying ability of the issuing insurance company.

Insurance products are offered through the insurance business 210 Financial. 210 Financial is also an Investment Advisory practice that offers products and services through AE Wealth Management, LLC (AEWM), a Registered Investment Advisor. AEWM does not offer insurance products. The insurance products offered by 210 Financial are not subject to Investment Advisor requirements

CHAPTER 2

Taxes

W here to begin with taxes? Perhaps by acknowledging we all bear responsibility for the resources we share. Roads, bridges, schools ... it is the patriotic duty of every American to pay their fair share of taxes. Many would agree with me, though, while they don't mind paying their fair share, they're not interested in paying one cent more than that!

Now, just talking taxes probably takes your mind to April—tax season. You are probably thinking about all the forms you collect and how you file. Perhaps you are thinking about your certified public accountant, or another qualified tax professional, and saying to yourself, "I've already got taxes taken care of, thanks!"

However, what I see when people come into my office is that their relationship with their tax professional is purely a January through April relationship. That means they may have a tax professional, but not a tax *planner*.

What I mean is tax planning extends beyond filing taxes. In April, we are required to settle our accounts with the IRS to make sure we have paid up on our bill or to even the score if we have overpaid. But real tax planning is about making each financial move in a way that allows you to keep the most money in your pocket and out of Uncle Sam's.

Now, as a caveat, I want to emphasize I am neither a CPA nor a tax planner, but I see the way taxes affect my clients, and I have plenty of experience helping clients implement tax-efficient strategies in their retirement plans in conjunction with their tax professionals.

Ahh, taxes. . .the only thing in this life that seems to be certain. Taxes have been and likely will be a large part of each of our lives until death do us part. And in some cases, even after you die. We often accepted the wisdom handed down by others during our younger years and invested our money in tax-deferred accounts. These vehicles include 401(k)s and IRAs. With those, we did not worry about paying the tax until we retired and would sometimes hear that we would most likely be in a lower tax bracket later in life. However, we are finding out that this strategy contains flaws.

We are living in a time of unprecedented government spending and national debt. At the time we published this book, the national debt approached $30,000,000,000,000. Can you even believe it? What's with all those zeroes? Well, that is $30 trillion, an incomprehensible number. We are also living among an aging population and drawing upon social programs like Social Security and Medicare at rates never seen in this country.

What do you think the government's solution will be? The programs you and I looked forward to as part of our retirement face some severe headwinds. They are largely funded from taxes directly from you, the American taxpayer. So, let me ask you, do you think taxes are going up in the future, or are they going down? I think it will be a losing argument to try and convince anyone that taxes are going down.

It is especially important to me to help my clients develop tax-efficient strategies in their retirement plans because each dollar they can keep in their pockets is a dollar we can put to work.

So, what should you be doing? Well, the first thing is to remind yourself that the money you have in your 401(k) and your IRA is not all yours. Wait, what?! "Phil, are you telling me that the money that I worked so hard to save and invest isn't all mine?" That is exactly right. You have a partner in those accounts, and that partner can be very stingy. The biggest problem is that your partner gets to determine how much of "your money" they get to take. Who is this partner? It is the tax man, the IRS. There is a part of your money that the government controls. If politicians feel the government needs more money, they just simply raise tax rates and poof, there goes more of your money. If they decide they want to be generous (fat chance, some say), then you get to keep more of your hard-earned dollars.

Here's the good news: strategies exist, including Roth IRAs and Roth IRA conversions, that allow you to help reduce the amount of your money you'll pay in taxes. By constructing a tax plan for your money, you can potentially save thousands of dollars, if not hundreds of thousands over your lifetime, that would have otherwise gone to pay taxes rather than your income obligations.

Here is a question for you: Do you want some control over how much you get to keep, or would you rather let the government control your financial future? Construct a plan, do it now, and make sure your plan incorporates methods designed to retain more of your money for you and your family. It is possible, but you have to take control. You must make, and follow, a plan.

This bears repeating: it is especially important to me to help my clients develop tax-efficient strategies in their retirement plans because each dollar they can keep in their pockets is a dollar we can put to work.

The Fed

Now, in the United States, taxes can be a rather uncertain proposition. Depending on who is in the White House and which party controls Congress, we might be tempted to assume tax rates could either decline or increase in the next four to eight years accordingly. However, there is one (large!) factor we, as a nation, must confront: the national debt.

Currently, according to USDebtClock.org, we are over $31,000,000,000,000 in debt and climbing. That's $31 *trillion* with a "T." With just $1 trillion, you could park it in the bank at a zero percent interest rate and spend more than $54 million every day for fifty years without hitting a zero balance.

Even if Congress got a handle and stopped that debt from its daily compound, divided by each taxpayer, we each would owe about $246,000. So, will that be check, cash, or Venmo?[18]

My point here isn't to give you anxiety. I'm just cautioning you that even with the rosiest of outlooks on our personal income tax rates, none of us should count on low tax rates for the long term. Instead, you and your network of professionals (tax, legal, and financial) should constantly be looking for ways to take advantage of tax-saving opportunities as they come. After all, the best "luck" is when proper planning meets opportunity.

So, how can we get started?

Know Your Limits

One of the foundational pieces of tax planning is knowing what tax bracket you are in, based on your income after subtracting pre-tax or untaxed assets. Your income taxes are based on your taxable income.

One reason to know your taxable income and your income tax rate is so you can see how far away you are from the next lower or higher tax bracket. This is particularly important when it comes to decisions such as gifting and Roth IRA rollovers.

For instance, when confronting the 2022 federal income tax return they filed in 2023, Mallory and Ralph's taxable income is just over $345,000, putting them in the 32 percent tax bracket and about $4,900 above the upper end of the 24 percent tax bracket. They have already maxed out their retirement funds' tax-exempt contributions for the year. Their daughter, Gloria, is a sophomore in college. This couple could

---

[18] usdebtclock.org.

shave a considerable amount off their tax bill if they use the $4,900 to help Gloria out with groceries and school— something they were likely to do, anyway, but now can deliberately be put to work for them in their overall financial strategy.

Now, I use Mallory and Ralph only as an example—your circumstances are probably different—but I think this nicely illustrates the way planning ahead for taxes can save you money.

Assuming a Lower Tax Rate

Many people anticipate being in a lower tax bracket in retirement. It makes sense: You won't be contributing to retirement funds; you'll be drawing from them. And you won't have all those work expenses—work clothes, transportation, lunch meetings, etc.

Yet, do you really plan on changing your lifestyle after retirement? Do you plan to cut down on the number of times you eat out, scale back vacations, and skimp on travel?

What I see in my office is many couples spend more in the first few years, or maybe the first decade, of retirement. Sure, that may taper off later on, but usually only just in time for their budget to be hit with greater health and long-term care expenses. Do you see where this is going? Many people plan as though their taxable income will be lower in retirement and are surprised when the tax bills come in and look more or less the same as they used to. It's better to plan for the worst and hope for the best, wouldn't you agree?

401(k)/IRA

One sometimes-unexpected piece of tax planning in retirement concerns your 401(k) or IRA. Most of us have one of these accounts or an equivalent. Throughout our working lives, we pay in, dutifully socking away a portion of our earnings in these tax-deferred accounts. There's the rub: tax-deferred. Not tax-free. Very rarely is anything free of taxation when you get down to it. Using 401(k)s and IRAs in retirement is no different. The taxes the government deferred when you were in your working years are now coming due, and you will pay taxes on that income at whatever your current tax rate is.

Just to ensure Uncle Sam gets his due, the government also has a required minimum distribution, or RMD, rule. Beginning at age seventy-three, you are required to withdraw a certain minimum amount every year from your 401(k) or IRA, or else you will face a 50 percent tax penalty on any RMD monies you should have withdrawn but didn't—and that's on top of income tax.

Of course, there is also the Roth account. You can think of the difference between a Roth and a traditional retirement account as the difference between taxing the seed and taxing the harvest. Because Roths are funded with post-tax dollars, there aren't tax penalties for early withdrawals of the principal nor are there taxes on the growth after you reach age fifty-nine-and-one-half. Perhaps best of all, there are no RMDs. Of course, you must own a Roth account for a minimum of five years before you are able to take advantage of all its features.

This is one more area where it pays to be aware of your tax bracket. Some people may find it advantageous to "convert" their traditional retirement account funds to Roth account funds in a year during which they are in a lower tax bracket. Others may opt to put any excess RMDs from their traditional retirement accounts into other products, like stocks or insurance.

Does that make your head spin? Understandable. That's why it's so important to work with a financial professional and tax planner who can help you not only execute these sorts of tax-efficient strategies but also help you understand what you are doing and why.

CHAPTER 3

Market Volatility

U p and down. Roller coaster. Merry-go-round. Bulls and bears. Peak-to-trough.

Sound familiar? This is the language we use to talk about the stock market. With volatility and spikes, even our language is jarring, bracing, and vivid.

Still, financial strategies tend to revolve around market-based products, for good reasons. For one thing, there is no other financial class that packs the same potential for growth, pound for pound, as stock-based products. Because of growth potential, inflation protection, and new opportunities, it may be unwise to avoid the market entirely.

However, along with the potential for growth is the potential for loss. Many of the people I see in my office come in still feeling a bit burned from the market drama of 2000 to 2010. That was a rough stretch, and many of us are once-bitten-twice-shy investors, right?

So how do we balance these factors? How do we try to satisfy both the need for protection and the need for growth?

For one thing, it is important to recognize the value of diversity. Now, I'm not just talking about the diversity of assets among different kinds of stocks, or even different kinds of stocks and bonds. That's only one kind of diversity; while important, both stocks and bonds, though different, are both still market-based products. Most market-based products, even within a diverse portfolio, tend to rise or lower as a whole, just like an incoming tide. Therefore, a portfolio diverse in only market-sourced products won't automatically protect your assets during times when the market declines.

In addition to the sort of "horizontal diversity" you have by purchasing a variety of stocks and bonds from different companies, I also suggest you think about "vertical diversity," or diversity among asset classes. This means having different product types, including securities products, bank products, and insurance products—with varying levels of growth potential, liquidity, and protection—all in accordance with your unique situation, goals, and needs.

Market volatility is as natural as the sun rising in the morning. Since the creation of the stock market, such turbulence has persisted, and it will conceivably continue in perpetuity. The problem with some people is that they let their emotions take over instead of having a plan.

I believe plans should welcome market volatility. It will attempt to capitalize on movement in the market, so it can potentially play to your advantage and not to your detriment. Without a plan, the market swings could allow your emotions to drive your investment philosophy. Often, that does not end well.

The Color of Money

When you're looking at the overall diversity of your portfolio, part of the equation is knowing which products fit in what category: what has liquidity, what has protection, and what has growth potential.

Before we dive in, keep in mind these aren't absolutes. You might think of liquidity, growth, and protection as primary colors. While some products will look pretty much yellow, red, or blue, others will have a mix of characteristics, making them more green, orange, or purple.

Growth

I like to think of the growth category as red. It's powerful, it's somewhat volatile, and it's also the category where we have the greatest opportunities for growth and loss. Often, products in the growth category will have a good deal of liquidity but very little protection. These are our market-based products and strategies, and we think of them mostly in shades of red and orange, to designate their growth and liquidity. This is a good place to be when you're young—think fast cars and flashy leather jackets—but its allure often wanes as you move closer to retirement. Examples of "red" products include:

- Stocks
- Equities
- Exchange-traded funds
- Mutual funds
- Corporate bonds
- Real estate investment trusts
- Speculations
- Alternative investments

Liquidity

Yellow is my liquid category color. I typically recommend having at least enough yellow money to cover six months' to a year's worth of expenses in case of emergency. Yellow assets don't need a lot of growth potential; they just need to be readily available when we need them. The "yellow" category includes assets like:

- Cash
- Money market accounts

Protection

The color of protection, to me, is blue. Tranquil, peaceful, sure, even if it lacks a certain amount of flash. This is the direction I like to see people generally move toward as they're nearing retirement. The red, flashy look of stock market returns and the risk of possible overnight losses is less attractive as we near retirement and look for more consistency and reliability. While this category doesn't come with a lot of liquidity, the products here are backed by an insurance company, a bank, or a government entity. "Blue" products include things such as:

- Certificates of deposit (backed by banks)
- Government-based bonds (backed by the U.S. government)
- Life insurance (backed by insurance companies)
- Annuities (backed by insurance companies)

One way to plan for market volatility is to have a retirement income plan, which enables you to set aside dollars unimpacted by the market. This can buy you time on your market-driven dollars. It can help you ride the market's ups and downs and hopefully prevent irrational, emotional decisions that could negatively affect your long-term financial stability.

401(k)s

I want to take a second to specifically address a product many retirees will be using to build their retirement income: the 401(k) and other retirement accounts. Any of these retirement accounts (IRAs, 401(k)s, 403(b)s, etc.) are basically "tax wrappers." What do I mean by that? Well, depending on your plan provider, a 401(k) could include target-date funds, passively managed products, stocks, bonds, mutual funds, or even variable, fixed, and fixed index annuities, all collected in one place and governed by rules (a.k.a. the "tax wrapper"). These rules govern how much money you can put inside, what ways you can put it in, when you will pay taxes on it, and when you can take the money out. Inside the 401(k), each of the products inside the "tax wrapper" might have its own fees or commissions, in addition to the management fee you pay on the 401(k) itself.

Dollar-Cost Averaging

With 401(k)s and other market-based retirement products, when you are investing for the long term, dollar-cost averaging is a concept that can work in your favor. When the market is trending up, if you are consistently paying in money, month over month, great; your investments can grow, and you are adding to your assets. When the market takes a dip, no problem; your dollars buy more shares at a lower price. At some point, we hope the market will rebound, in which case your shares can grow and possibly be more valuable than they were before. This concept is what we call "dollar-cost averaging." While it can't ensure a profit or guarantee against losses, it's a time-tested strategy for investing in a volatile market.

However, when you are in retirement, this strategy may work against you. You may have heard of "reverse" dollar-cost averaging. Before, when the market lost ground, you were "bargain-shopping"; your dollars purchased more assets at a reduced price. When you are in retirement, you are no longer the purchaser; you are selling. So, in a down market, you have to sell more assets to make the same amount of money as what you made in a favorable market.

I've had lots of people step into my office to talk to me about this, emphasizing, "my advisor says the market always bounces back, and I have to just hold on for the long term."

There's some basis for this thinking; thus far, the market has always rebounded to higher heights than before. But this is no guarantee, and the prospect of potentially higher returns in five years may not be very helpful in retirement if you are relying on the income from those returns to pay this month's electric bill, for example.

Is There a "Perfect" Product?

To bring us back around to the discussion of protection, growth, and liquidity, the ideal product would be a "ten" in all three categories, right? Completely guaranteed, doubling in size every few years, and accessible whenever you want. Does such a product exist? Anyone who says "yes" is either ignorant or malevolent.

Instead of running in circles looking for that perfect product, the silver bullet, the unicorn of financial strategies, it's more important to circle back to the concept of a balanced, asset-diverse portfolio.

This is why your interests may be best served when you work with a trusted financial professional who knows what various financial products can do and how to use them in your personal retirement strategy.

CHAPTER 4

Retirement Income

Retirement. For many of us, it's what we've saved for and dreamed of, pinning our hopes to a magical someday. Is that someday full of traveling? Is it filled with grandkids? Gardening? Maybe your fondest dream is simply never having to work again, never having to clock in or be accountable to someone else.

Your ability to do these things all hinges on *income*. Without the money to support these dreams, even a basic level of work-free lifestyle is unsustainable. That's why planning for your income in retirement is so foundational. But where do we begin?

It's easy to feel overwhelmed by this question. Some may feel the urge to amass a large lump sum and then try to put it all in one product—insurance, investments, liquid assets—to provide all the growth, liquidity, and income they need. Instead, I think you need a more balanced approach. After all, retirement planning isn't magic. Like I mention elsewhere, there is no single product that can be all things to all people (or even all things to one person). No approach works unilaterally for everyone. That's why it's important to talk to a financial professional who can help you lay down the basics and take you step-by-step through the process. Not only will you have the assurance you have addressed the areas you need to, but you will also have an ally who can help you break down the process and help keep you from feeling overwhelmed.

Sources of Income

Thinking of all the pieces of your retirement expenses might be intimidating. But, like cleaning out a junk drawer or revisiting that garage remodel, once you have laid everything out, you can begin to sort things into categories.

Once you have a good overall picture of where your expenses will lie, you can start stacking up the resources to cover them.

Social Security

Social Security is a guaranteed, inflation-protected federal insurance program playing a significant part in most of our retirement plans. From delaying until you've reached full retirement age or beyond to examining spousal benefits, as I discuss elsewhere in this book, there is plenty you can do to try to make the most of this monthly benefit. As with all your retirement income sources, it's important to consider how to make this resource stretch to provide the most bang and buck for your situation.

Pension

Another generally reliable source of retirement income for you might be a pension, if you are one of the lucky people who still has one.

If you don't have a pension, go ahead and skim on to the next section. If you do have a pension, keep on reading.

Because your pension can be such a central piece of your retirement income plan, you will want to put some thought into answering basic questions about it.

How well is your pension funded? Since the heyday of the pension plan, companies and governments have neglected to fund their pension obligations, causing a persistent problem with this otherwise reliable asset.

Consider the factors at play, though. Pensions had been underfunded and gained a boost from strong market performance in 2021. What happens to the solvency of those pension funds if the market declines?

It can be worthwhile to keep tabs on your pension's health and know what your options are for withdrawing your pension. If you have already retired and made those decisions, this may be a foregone conclusion. If not, it pays to know what you can expect and what decisions you can make, such as taking spousal options to cover your husband or wife if he or she outlives you.

Also, some companies are incentivizing lump-sum payouts of pensions to reduce the companies' payment liabilities. If that's the case with your employer, talk to your financial professional to see if it might be prudent to do something like that or if it might be better to stick with lifetime payments or other options.

Your 401(k) and IRA

One "modern way" to save for retirement is in a 401(k) or IRA (or their nonprofit or governmental equivalents). These tax-advantaged accounts are, in my opinion, a poor substitute for pensions, but one of the biggest disservices we do to ourselves is to not take full advantage of them in the first place. According to one article, only 32 percent of Americans invest in a 401(k), though 59 percent of employed Americans have access to a 401(k) benefit option.[19]

Also, if you have changed jobs over the years, do the work of tracking down any benefits from your past employers. You might have an IRA here or a 401(k) there; keep track of those so you can pull them together and look at those assets when you're ready to look at establishing sources of retirement income.

---

[19] Amin Dabit. personalcapital.com. April 1, 2021. "The Average 401k Balance by Age." https://www.personalcapital.com/blog/retirement-planning/average-401k-balance-age/

Do You Have...

- Life insurance?
- Annuities?
- Long-term care insurance?
- Any passive income sources?
- Stock and bond portfolios?
- Liquid assets? (What's in your bank account?)
- Alternative investments?
- Rental properties?

It's important, if you are going through the work of sitting with a financial professional, to look at your full retirement income picture and pull together *all* your assets, no matter how big or small. From the free insurance policy offered at your bank to the sizable investment in your brother-in-law's modestly successful furniture store, you want to have a good idea of where your money is.

Some of the most rewarding moments of my career come from sitting with a new couple. We first make small talk because I want to learn about their experiences, aspirations, and how they envision their retirement. While the stories always vary because they are personal in nature, the hopes and dreams they express are similar to other clients and sometimes similar to my own.

Many have worked hard, saved hard, and now want to play hard in retirement. What holds them back in some cases is the lack of planning. It's possible sometimes, after examining portfolios, to ask the question, "Why aren't you retired?"

If they have the means to retire but look astonished by the question, I sometimes hear an answer: "because we can't afford to retire." This is when I am reminded of my calling in life, to help people plan for all retirement considerations and, if possible, show them a path that allows them to cease working. The responses can be priceless, including one instance when a client retrieved his cell phone, called his boss, and relayed his decision to retire right then and there.

This doesn't happen because I wave some magic wand or sprinkle an account statement with pixie dust. Nor is it possible for everyone I see. But I cannot understate the value of a thorough retirement income plan and the possibilities that sometimes unfold when people better understand how their savings, and all the sacrifices they made to build that nest egg, can work for them in retirement. The possibilities can be enlightening.

Retirement Income Needs

How much income will you need in retirement? How do you determine that? A lot of people work toward a random number, thinking, "If I can just have a million dollars, I'll be comfortable in retirement!" Don't get me wrong; it is possible to save up a lot of money and then retire in the hopes you can keep your monthly expenses lower than some set estimation. But I think this carries a general risk of running out of money. Instead, I work with my clients to find out what their current and projected income needs are and then work from there to see how we might cover any gaps between what they have and what they want.

Goals and Dreams

I like to start with your pie in the sky. Do you find yourself planning for your vacations more thoroughly than you do your retirement? It's not uncommon for Americans to spend more time planning our vacations than we spend planning our retirements. Maybe it's because planning a vacation is less stressful: Having a week at the beach go awry is, well, a walk on the beach compared to running out of money in retirement. Whatever the case, perhaps it would be better if you thought of your retirement as a vacation in and of itself—no clocking in, no boss, no overtime. If you felt unlimited by financial strain, what would you do?

Would an endless vacation for you mean Paris and Rome? Would it mean mentoring at children's clubs or serving at the local soup kitchen? Or maybe it would mean deepening your ties to those immediately around you—neighbors, friends, and family. Maybe it would mean more time to take part in the hobbies and activities you love. Have you been considering a second (or even third) act as a small-business owner, turning a hobby or passion into a revenue source?

This is your time to daydream and answer the question: If you could do anything, what would you do?

After that, it's a matter of putting a dollar amount on it. What are the costs of round-the-world travel? One couple I know said their highest priority in retirement was being able to take each of their grandchildren on a cross-country vacation every year. That's a pretty specific goal—one that is reasonably easy to nail down a budget for.

Current Budget

Compiling a current expense report is one of the trickiest pieces of retirement preparation. Many people assume the expenses of their lives in retirement will be different—lower. After all, there will be no drive to work, no need for a formal wardrobe, and, perhaps most impactful of all, no more saving for retirement!

Yet, we often underestimate our daily spending habits. That's why I typically ask my clients to bring in their bank statements for the past year—they are reflective of your *actual* spending, not just what you think you're spending.

The best way to assess your monthly income needs is to simply track your expenses for a month and write them down. Now, don't cheat. Reconcile every purchase on pen and paper, or keep your tab in a computer file. Whatever works for you.

Everything you pay for, from buying a soda to paying the light bill, gets recorded. By writing it down, or typing it in, this will become the budget from which we build your plan. We always say, "don't let your outgo become your downfall." You must know where your money is going.

I can't count the number of times I have sat with a couple, asked them about their spending, and heard them throw out a number that seemed incredibly low. When I ask them where the number came from, they usually say they estimated based on their total bills. Yet, our spending is so much more than our mortgage, utilities, cable, phone, car, grocery, or credit card bills.

"What about clothes?" I ask, "Or dining out? What about gifts and coffees and last-minute birthday cards?" That's when the lights come on.

This is why I suggest collecting a year's worth of information. There is usually no such thing as a one-time purchase. Did you buy new furniture? Even if that is a rarity, do you think that will be the last time you *ever* buy furniture?

Many times when I ask a client what their monthly budget is, they freeze and even look shocked to some extent. They simply do not know! One of the key factors of a good retirement plan is to know where your money is going, be it a loan payment, a utility bill, prescription drugs, online or streaming subscriptions, support for a family member, or a miscellaneous expense.

If you do this, you may learn that you are spending more than you thought, sometimes on things you do not need or even use. You can stretch your retirement dollars by adjusting or eliminating some payments. Additional funds you create could potentially allow you to do things you thought you would never do, like travel, contribute to charity, or enjoy activities you ruled out as too expensive.

Another hefty expense is spending on the kids. Many of the couples I work with are quick to help their adult children, whether it's something like letting them live in the basement, paying for college, babysitting, paying an occasional bill, or contributing to a grandchild's college fund. They aren't alone— 79 percent of Americans in 2018 said they had provided financial support for an adult child. And it's not unlikely for some parents to tap into their retirement funds to do so.[20]

My clients sometimes protest that what they do for their grown children can stop in retirement. They don't *need* to help. But I get it. Parents like to feel needed. And, while you never want to neglect saving for retirement in favor of taking on financial risks (like your child's student debt), the parents who help their adult children do so in part because it helps them feel fulfilled.

When it comes down to expenses, including (and especially) spending on your family, don't make your initial calculations based on what you *could* whittle your budget down to if you *had* to. Instead, start from where you are. Who wants to live off a bare-bones bank account in retirement?

Other Expenses

Once you have nailed down your current budget and your dreams or goals for retirement, there are a few other outstanding pieces to think about—some expenses many people don't take the time to consider before making and executing a plan. But I'm assuming you want to get it right, so let's take a look.

Housing

Do you know where you want to live in retirement? This makes up a substantial piece of your income puzzle—since the typical American household owns a home, and it's generally their largest asset.

Some people prefer to live right where they are for as long as they can. Others have been waiting for retirement to pull the

[20] Lorie Konish. CNBC. October 2, 2018. "Parents Spend Twice as Much on Adult Children than They Save for Retirement."
https://www.cnbc.com/2018/10/02/parents-spend-twice-as-much-on-adult-children-than-saving-for-retirement.html

trigger on an ambitious move, like purchasing a new house, or even downsizing. Whatever your plans and whatever your reasons, there are quite a few things to consider.

Mortgage

Do you still have a mortgage? What may have been a nice tax boon in your working years could turn into a financial burden in your retirement. After all, when you are on a limited income, a mortgage is just one more bill sapping your financial strength. It is something to put some thought into, whether you plan to age in place or are considering moving to your dream home, buying a house out of state, or living in a retirement community.

Upkeep and Taxes

A house without a mortgage still requires annual taxes. While it's tempting to think of this as a once-a-year expense, when you have limited earning potential, your annual tax bill might be something into which you should put a little more forethought.

The costs of homeownership aren't just monetary. When you find yourself dealing with more house than you need, it can drain your time and energy. From keeping clutter at bay to keeping the lawn mower running, upkeep can be extensive and expensive. For some, that's a challenge they heartily accept and can comfortably take on. For others, the idea of yard work or cleaning an area larger than they need feels foolish.

For instance, Peggy discovered after her knee replacement that most of her house was inaccessible to her when she was laid up.

"It felt ridiculous to pay someone else to dust and vacuum a house I was only living in 40 percent of!"

Practicality and Adaptability

Erik and Magda are looking to retire within the next two decades. They just sold their old three-bedroom ranch-style house. Their twins are in high school, and the couple has wanted to "upgrade" for years. Now they live in a gorgeous 1940s three-story house with all the kitchen space they ever wanted, five sprawling bedrooms, and a library and media room for themselves and their children. Within months of moving in, the couple realized a house perfect for their active teens would no longer be perfect for them in five to fifteen years.

"We are paying the mortgage for this house, but we've started saving for the next one," said Magda, "because who wants to climb two flights of stairs to their bedroom when they're seventy-eight?"

Others I know have encountered a similar situation in their personal lives. After a health crisis, one couple found the luxurious tub for two they toiled to install had become a specter of a bad slip and a potential safety risk. It's important to think through what your physical reality could be. I always emphasize to my clients that they should plan for whatever their long-term future might hold, but it's amazing how many people don't give it much thought.

Contracts and Regulations

If you are looking into a cross-country move, be aware of new tax tables or local ordinances in the area where you are looking to move. After all, you don't want to experience sticker-shock when you are looking at downsizing or reducing your bills in retirement.

Along the same lines, if you are moving into a retirement community, be sure to look at the fine print. What happens if you must move into a different situation for long-term care? Will you be penalized? Will you be responsible for replacing your slot in the community? What are all the fees, and what do they cover?

Inflation

As I write this in 2022, America has experienced a wave of inflation following a lengthy period of low inflation. Inflation zoomed to 9.1 percent in June 2022, its highest mark since November 1981.[21]

Core inflation is yet another measurement that excludes goods with prices that tend to be more volatile, such as food and energy costs. Core inflation for a 12-month period ending in December 2022 was 5.7 percent. It so happened energy prices rose7.3 percent over that timeframe.[22]

However, inflation isn't a one-time bump; it has a cumulative effect. Again, that can impact the price of groceries greater than other goods. Even with relatively low inflation over the past few decades, an item you bought in 1997 for two dollars will cost about $3.70 today.[23] Want to go to a show? A $20 ticket in 1997 would cost $41.24 in 2022.[24]

What if, in retirement, we hit a stretch like the late seventies and early eighties, when annual inflation rates of 10 percent became the norm? It may be wise to consider some extra padding in your retirement income plan to account for any potential increase in inflation in the future.

---

[21] tradingeconomics.com. 2022 Data/2023 Forecast/1914-2021 Historical. "United States Inflation Rate" https://tradingeconomics.com/united-states/inflation-cpi

[22] U.S. Inflation Calculator. "United States Core Inflation Rates (1957-2022)" https://www.usinflationcalculator.com/inflation/united-states-core-inflation-rates/

[23] In2013dollars.com. "$2 in 1997 is worth $3.70 today" https://www.in2013dollars.com/us/inflation/1997?amount=2

[24] In2013dollars.com "Admission to movies, theaters, and concerts priced at $20 in 1997>$40.34 in 2022" https://www.in2013dollars.com/Admission-to-movies,-theaters,-and-concerts/price-inflation

Aging

Also, in the expense category, think about longevity. We all hope to age gracefully. However, it's important to face the prospect of aging with a sense of realism.

The elephant in the room for many families is long-term care: No one wants to admit they will likely need it, but estimates say as many as 70 percent of us will.[25] Aging is a significant piece of retirement income planning because you'll want to figure out how to set aside money for your care, either at home or away from it. The more comfortable you get with discussing your wishes and plans with your loved ones, the easier planning for the financial side of it can be.

I discuss health care and potential long-term care costs in more detail elsewhere in this book, but suffice it to say nursing home care tends to be very expensive and typically isn't something you get to choose when you will need.

It isn't just the costs of long-term care that pose a concern in living longer. It's also about covering the possible costs of everything else associated with living longer. For instance, if Henry retires from his job as a biochemical engineer at age sixty-five, perhaps he planned to have a very decent income for twenty years, until age eighty-five. But what if he lives until he's ninety-five? That's a whole third—ten years—more of personal income he will need.

Putting It All Together

Whew! So, you have pulled together what you have, and you have a pretty good idea of where you want to be. Now your financial professional and you can go about the work of arranging what assets you *have* to cover what you *need*—and how you might try to cover any gaps.

---

[25] Moll Law Group. 2021. "The Cost of Long-Term Care." https://www.molllawgroup.com/the-cost-of-long-term-care.html

Like the proverbial man in the Bible who built his house on a rock, I like to help my clients figure out how to cover their day-to-day living expenses—their needs—with insurance and other guaranteed income sources like pensions and Social Security.

At 210 Financial, we help clients plan for retirement by creating a "retirement blueprint." Why do we call it a blueprint? Because a blueprint is the foundational piece of any building project. For a building, the blueprint informs where to put the foundation, how thick the walls need to be, how much concrete needs to be poured, where to put the bathroom, how to install the roof, and so on.

The same is true for a financial blueprint. It will tell us how much your expenses are, where the income is going to come from, how much investment risk you have or should have, and what happens if a significant medical situation develops. A good solid blueprint is a key to a good solid retirement plan.

Again, you should keep in mind there isn't one single financial vehicle, asset, or source to fill all your needs, and that's okay. One of the challenges of planning for your income in retirement concerns figuring out what products and strategies to use. You can release some of that stress when you accept the fact you will probably need a diverse portfolio—potentially with bonds, stocks, insurance, and other income sources—not just one massive money pile.

One way to help shore up your income gaps is by working with your financial professional and a qualified tax advisor to mitigate your tax exposure. If you have a 401(k) or IRA, a tax advisor in your corner can help you figure out how and when to take distributions from your account in a way that doesn't push you into a higher tax bracket. Or you might learn how to use tax-advantaged bonds more effectively. Effective tax planning isn't necessarily about "adding" to your income. Especially regarding retirement, it's less about what you make than it is about what you keep. Paying a lower tax bill keeps more money in your pocket, which is where you want it when it comes to retirement income.

Now you can look at ways to cover your remaining retirement goals. Are there products like long-term care insurance specific to a certain kind of expense you anticipate? Is there a particular asset you want to use for your "play" money—money for trips and gifts for the grandkids? Is there any way you can portion off money for those charitable legacy plans?

Once you have analyzed your income wants, needs, and the assets to realistically cover them, you may have a gap. The masterstroke of a competent financial professional will be to help you figure out how you will cover that gap. Will you need to cut out a round of golf a week? Maybe skip the new car? Or will you need to take more substantial action?

One way to cover an income gap is to consider working longer or even part-time before retirement and even after that magical calendar date. This may not be the best "plan" for you; disabilities, work demands, and physical or emotional limitations can hinder the best-laid plans to continue working. However, if it is physically possible for you, this is one considerable way to help your assets last, for more than one reason.

In fact, about one in five Americans are still working past age sixty-five. This is a record percentage in the past half-century. While some do list their personal finances as a reason for staying on the job, others do so to avoid feeling bored in retirement, among other reasons.[26]

---

[26] Associated Press. October 9, 2018. "1 in 5 Americans over 65 are Still Waiting to Retire." https://nypost.com/2018/10/09/1-in-5-americans-over-65-are-still-waiting-to-retire/

When you're retired, you no longer have an employer paying you a steady check. It is up to you to make sure you have saved and planned for the income you need.

CHAPTER 5

Social Security

Social Security is often the foundation of retirement income. Backed by the strength of the U.S. Treasury, it provides perhaps the most dependable paycheck you will have in retirement.

The day I got my first paycheck was one of the greatest days of my life. It meant freedom to me. I was sixteen years old and I had started my illustrious career at a local restaurant washing dishes. I was on my way in life. Minimum wage in those days was $3.35 per hour, and I had worked ten hours for an amazing $33.50 that first week! Well, so I thought.

Wait. What? Taxes? What does that mean? Why is my check smaller? Who took my money? This provided me with my first lesson in financial planning. I realized right then and there that I was not fully in charge of my life and that without some kind of guidance, I was just floating downstream, subject to the whims of whatever, or should I say whoever, wanted to control my money.

I carried that lesson into my career and I have become passionate about helping people retain more of their hard-earned money. I know more about the whims (typically those of politicians) that prompt changes to our tax structure while attempting to help clients fulfill their retirement dreams.

This includes keeping close tabs on one of the programs to which a large portion of what you pay in taxes gets funneled, Social Security. You are likely paying into the grand old Social Security system from the time you receive your first paycheck, including my position as a dishwasher. What grew and developed out of the pressures of the Great Depression has become one of the most popular government programs in the country, and, if you pay in for the equivalent of ten years or more, you, too, can benefit from the Social Security program.

Now, before we get into the nitty-gritty of Social Security, I'd like to address a current concern: Will Social Security still be there for you when you reach retirement age?

The Future of Social Security

This question is ever-present as headlines trumpet an underfunded Social Security program, alongside the sea of baby boomers who are retiring in droves and the comparatively smaller pool of younger people who are bearing the responsibility of funding the system.

The Social Security Administration itself acknowledges this concern as each Social Security statement now contains a link to its website (ssa.gov) and a page entitled, "Will Social Security Be There For Me?"

Just a reminder, as if you needed one, that nothing in life is guaranteed. Additionally, depending on who you're listening to, Social Security funds may run low before 2034 thanks to the financial instability and government spending that accompanied the 2020 COVID-19 pandemic.

Before you get too discouraged, though, here are a few thoughts to keep you going:

- Even if the program is only paying 78 cents on the dollar for scheduled benefits, 78 percent is notably not zero.
- The Social Security Administration has made changes in the distant and near past to protect the fund's solvency, including increasing retirement ages and striking certain filing strategies.
- There are many changes Congress could make, and lawmakers are currently discussing how to fix the

system, such as further increasing full retirement age and eligibility.

- One thing no one is seriously discussing? Reneging on current obligations to retirees or the soon-to-retire.

Take heart. The real answer to the question, "Will Social Security be there for me?" is still yes.

This question is an important one to consider when you look at how much we, as a nation, rely on this program. Did you know Social Security benefits replace about 40 percent of a person's original income when they retire?[27]

If you ask me, that's a pretty significant piece of your retirement income puzzle.

Another caveat? You may not realize this, but no one can legally "advise" you about your Social Security benefits.

"But, Phil," you may be thinking, "isn't that part of what you do? And what about that nice gentleman at the Social Security Administration office I spoke with on the phone?"

Don't get me wrong. Social Security Administration employees know their stuff. They are trained to know policies and programs, and they are usually pretty quick to tell you what you can and cannot do. But the government specifically stipulates, because Social Security is a benefit you alone have paid into and earned, your Social Security decisions, too, are yours alone.

When it comes to financial professionals, we can't push you in any direction, either, *but*—there's a big but here—working with a well-informed financial professional is still incredibly handy when it comes to your Social Security decisions. Why? Because someone who's worth his or her salt will know what withdrawal strategies might pertain to your specific situation and will ask questions that can help you determine what you are looking for when it comes to your Social Security.

---

27 Social Security Administration. "Learn About Social Security Programs." https://www.ssa.gov/planners/retire/r&m6.html

For instance, some people want the highest possible monthly benefit. Others want to start their benefits early, not always because of financial need. I heard about one man who called in to start his Social Security payments the day he qualified, just because he liked to think of it as the government paying back a debt it owed him, and he enjoyed the feeling of receiving a check from Uncle Sam.

Whatever your reasons, questions, or feelings regarding Social Security, the decision is yours alone; but working with a financial professional can help you put your options in perspective by showing you—both with industry knowledge and with proprietary software or planning processes— where your benefits fit into your overall strategy for retirement income.

One reason the federal government doesn't allow for "advice" related to Social Security, I suspect, is so no one can profit from giving you advice related to your Social Security benefit—or from providing any clarifications. Again, this is a sign of a good financial professional. Those who are passionate about their work will be knowledgeable about what benefit strategies might be to your advantage and will happily share those possible options with you.

Full Retirement Age

When it comes to Social Security, it seems like many people only think so far as "yes." They don't take the time to understand the various options available. Instead, because it is common knowledge you can begin your benefits at age sixty-two, that's what many of us do. While more people are opting to delay taking benefits, age sixty-two is still firmly the most popular age to start.[28]

---

[28] Chris Kissell. moneytalknews.com. January 20, 2021. "This Is When the Most People Start Taking Social Security." https://www.moneytalksnews.com/the-most-popular-age-for-claiming-social-security/

What many people fail to understand is, by starting benefits early, they may be leaving a lot of money on the table. You see, the Social Security Administration bases your monthly benefit on two factors: your earnings history and your full retirement age (FRA).

From your earnings history, they pull the thirty-five years you made the most money and use a mathematical indexing formula to figure out a monthly average from those years. If you paid into the system for less than thirty-five years, then every year you didn't pay in will be counted as a zero.

Once they have calculated what your monthly earning would be at FRA, the government then calculates what to put on your check based on how close you are to FRA. FRA was originally set at sixty-five, but, as the population aged and lifespans lengthened, the government shifted FRA later and later, based on an individual's year of birth. Check out the following chart to see when you will reach FRA.[29]

[29] Social Security Administration. "Full Retirement Age." https://www.ssa.gov/planners/retire/retirechart.html

Age to Receive Full Social Security Benefits*

(Called "full retirement age" [FRA] or "normal retirement age.")

Year of Birth*	FRA
1937 or earlier	65
1938	65 and 2 months
1939	65 and 4 months
1940	65 and 6 months
1941	65 and 8 months
1942	65 and 10 months
1943-1954	66
1955	66 and 2 months
1956	66 and 4 months
1957	66 and 6 months
1958	66 and 8 months
1959	66 and 10 months
1960 and later	67

If you were born on Jan. 1 of any year, you should refer to the previous year. (If you were born on the 1st of the month, we figure your benefit [and your full retirement age] as if your birthday was in the previous month.)

When you reach FRA, you are eligible to receive 100 percent of whatever the Social Security Administration says is your full monthly benefit.

Starting at age sixty-two, for every year before FRA you claim benefits, your monthly check is reduced by 5 percent or more. Conversely, for every year you delay taking benefits past FRA, your monthly benefit increases by 8 percent (until age seventy—after that, there is no monetary advantage to delaying Social Security benefits). While your circumstances and needs may vary, a lot of financial professionals still urge people to at least consider delaying until they reach age seventy.

Why wait?[30]

Taking benefits early could affect your monthly check by _____.								
62	63	64	65	FRA 66	67	68	69	70
-25 %	-20 %	-13.3 %	-6.7 %	0	+8 %	+16 %	+24 %	+32 %

My Social Security

If you are over age thirty, you have probably received a notice from the Social Security Administration telling you to activate something called "My Social Security." This is a handy way to learn more about your particular benefit options, to keep track of what your earnings record looks like, and to calculate the benefits you have accrued over the years.

Essentially, My Social Security is an online account you can activate to see what your personal Social Security picture looks like, which you can do at www.ssa.gov/myaccount. This can be extremely helpful when it comes to planning for income in retirement and figuring up the difference between your anticipated income versus anticipated expenses.

[30] Social Security Administration. April 2021. "Can You Take Your Benefits Before Full Retirement Age?"
https://www.ssa.gov/planners/retire/applying2.html

My Social Security is also helpful because it's a great way to see if there is a problem. For instance, I have heard of one woman who, through diligently checking her tax records against her Social Security profile, discovered her Social Security check was shortchanging her, based on her earnings history. After taking the discrepancy to the Social Security Administration, they sent her what they owed her in makeup benefits.

COLA

Social Security is a largely guaranteed piece of the retirement puzzle: If you get a statement that reads you should expect $1,000 a month, you can be sure you will receive $1,000 a month. But there is one variable detail, and that is something called the cost-of-living adjustment, or COLA.

The COLA is an increase in your monthly check meant to address inflation in everyday life. After all, your expenses will likely continue to experience inflation in retirement, but you will no longer have the opportunity for raises, bonuses, or promotions you had when you were working. Instead, Social Security receives an annual cost-of-living increase tied to the Department of Labor's Consumer Price Index for Urban Wage Earners and Clerical Workers, or CPI-W. If the CPI-W measurement shows inflation rose a certain amount for regular goods and services, then Social Security recipients will see that reflected in their COLA.

COLA adjustments have climbed as high as 14.3 percent (1980) and in 2023 reached 8.7 percent, the largest increase in more than forty years. But in a no- or low-inflation environment, such as in 2010, 2011, and 2016, Social Security recipients will not receive an adjustment.[31] Some view the COLA as a perk, bump, or bonus, but, in reality, it works more like this: Your mom sends you to the store with $2.50 for a gallon of milk. Milk costs exactly $2.50. The next week, you go

---

[31] ssa.gov. "Cost-Of-Living Adjustments" ssa.gov/oact/cola/colaseries.html

back with that same amount, but it is now $2.52 for a gallon, so you go back to Mom, and she gives you 2 cents. You aren't bringing home more milk—it just costs more money.

So the COLA is less about "making more money" and more about keeping seniors' purchasing power from eroding when inflation is a big factor, such as in 1975, when it was 8 percent![32] Still, don't let that detract from your enthusiasm about COLAs; after all, what if Mom's solution was: "Here's the same $2.50; try to find pennies from somewhere else to get that milk!"?

Spousal Benefits

We've talked about FRA, but another big Social Security decision involves spousal benefits.

If you or your spouse has a long stretch of zeros in your earnings history—perhaps if one of you stayed home for years, caring for children or sick relatives—you may want to consider filing for spousal benefits instead of filing on your own earnings history. A spousal benefit can be up to 50 percent of the primary wage earner's benefit at full retirement age.

To begin drawing a spousal benefit, you must be at least sixty-two years old, and the primary wage earner must have already filed for his or her benefit. While there are penalties for taking spousal benefits early, you cannot earn credits for delaying past full retirement age.[33]

Like I wrote, the spousal benefit can be a big deal for those who don't have a very long pay history, but it's important to weigh your own earned benefits against the option of withdrawing based on a fraction of your spouse's benefits.

To look at how this could play out, let's use a hypothetical couple: Mary Jane, who is sixty, and Peter, who is sixty-two.

---

[32] Social Security Administration. "Cost-Of-Living Adjustment (COLA) Information for 2021." https://www.ssa.gov/cola/
[33] Social Security Administration. "Retirement Planner: Benefits For You As A Spouse." https://www.ssa.gov/planners/retire/applying6.html

Let's say Peter's benefit at FRA, in his case sixty-seven, would be $1,600. If Peter begins his benefits right now, four years before FRA, his monthly check will be $1,200. If Mary Jane begins taking spousal benefits in two years at the earliest date possible, her monthly benefits will be reduced by 67.5 percent, to $520 per month (remember, at FRA, the most she can qualify for is half of Peter's FRA benefit).

What if Peter and Mary Jane both wait until FRA? At sixty-seven, Peter begins taking his full benefit of $1,600 a month. Two years later, when she reaches age sixty-seven, Mary Jane will qualify for $800 a month. By waiting until FRA, the couple's monthly benefit goes from $1,720 to $2,400.

What if Peter delays until age seventy to get his maximum possible benefit? For each year past FRA he delays, his monthly benefits increase by 8 percent. This means, at seventy, he could file for a monthly benefit of $2,015. However, delayed retirement credits do not affect spousal benefits, so as soon as Peter files at seventy, Mary Jane would also file (at age sixty-eight) for her maximum benefit of $800, so their highest possible combined monthly check is $2,815.[34]

When it comes to your Social Security benefits, you obviously will want to consider whether a monthly check based on a fraction of your spouse's earnings will be comparable to or larger than your own earnings history.

Divorced Spouses

There are a few considerations for those of us who have gone through a divorce. If you 1) were married for ten years or more *and* 2) have since been divorced for at least two years *and* 3) are unmarried *and* 4) your ex-spouse qualifies to begin Social Security, you qualify for a spousal benefit based on your ex-husband or ex-wife's earnings history at FRA. A divorced

---

[34] Office of the Chief Actuary. Social Security Administration. "Social Security Benefits: Benefits for Spouses." https://www.ssa.gov/OACT/quickcalc/spouse.html#calculator

spousal benefit is different from the married spousal benefit in one way: You don't have to wait for your ex-spouse to file before you can file yourself.[35]

For instance, Charles and Moira were married for fifteen years before their divorce, when he was thirty-six and she was forty. Moira has been remarried for twenty years, and, although Charles briefly remarried, his second marriage ended after a few years. Charles' benefits are largely calculated based on his many years of volunteering in schools, meaning his personal monthly benefit is close to zero.

Although Moira has deferred her retirement, opting to delay benefits until she is seventy, Charles can begin taking benefits calculated from Moira's work history at FRA as early as sixty-two. However, he will also have the option of waiting until FRA to collect the maximum, or 50 percent of Moira's earned monthly benefit at her FRA.

Widowed Spouses

If your marriage ended with the death of your spouse, you might claim a benefit for your spouse's earned income as his or her widow/widower, called a survivor's benefit. Unlike a spousal benefit or divorced benefits, if your husband or wife dies, you can claim his or her full benefit. Also, unlike spousal benefits, if you need to, you can begin taking income when you turn sixty. However, as with other benefit options, your monthly check will be permanently reduced for withdrawing benefits before FRA.

If your spouse began taking benefits before he or she died, you can't delay withdrawing your survivor's benefits to get delayed credits. The Social Security Administration maintains

---

35 Social Security Administration. "Retirement Planner: If You Are Divorced." https://www.ssa.gov/planners/retire/divspouse.html

you can only get as much from a survivor's benefit as your deceased spouse might have received, had he or she lived.[36]

Taxes, Taxes, Taxes

With Social Security, as with everything, it is important to consider taxes. It may be surprising, but your Social Security benefits are not tax-free. Despite having been taxed to accrue those benefits in the first place, you may have to pay Uncle Sam income taxes on up to 85 percent of your Social Security.

The Social Security Administration figures these taxes using what they call "the provisional income formula." Your provisional income formula differs from the adjusted gross income you use for your regular income taxes. Instead, to find out how much of your Social Security benefit is taxable, the Social Security Administration calculates it this way:

Provisional Income = Adjusted Gross Income + Nontaxable Interest + ½ of Social Security

See that piece about nontaxable interest? That generally means interest from government bonds and notes. It surprises many people that, although you may not pay taxes on those assets, their income will count against you when it comes to Social Security taxation.

Once you have figured out your provisional income (also called "combined income"), you can use the following chart to figure out your Social Security taxes.[37]

---

[36] Social Security Administration. "Social Security Benefit Amounts For The Surviving Spouse By Year Of Birth." https://www.ssa.gov/planners/survivors/survivorchartred.html
[37] Social Security Administration. "Benefits Planner: Income Taxes and Your Social Security Benefits." https://www.ssa.gov/planners/taxes.html

Taxes on Social Security		
Provisional Income = Adjusted Gross Income + Nontaxable Interest + ½ of Social Security		
If you are ____ and your provisional income is____, then...		Uncle Sam will tax ___ of your Social Security
Single	Married, filing jointly	
Less than $25,000	Less than $32,000	0%
$25,000 to $34,000	$32,000 to $44,000	Up to 50%
More than $34,000	More than $44,000	Up to 85%

This is one more reason it may benefit you to work with financial and tax professionals: They can look at your entire financial picture to make your overall retirement plan as tax-efficient as possible—including your Social Security benefit.

Working and Social Security: The Earnings Test

If you haven't reached FRA, but you started your Social Security benefits and are still working, things get a little hairy.

Because you have started Social Security payments, the Social Security Administration will pay out your benefits (at that reduced rate, of course, because you haven't reached your FRA). Yet, because you are working, the organization must also withhold from your check to add to your benefits, which you are already collecting. See how this complicates matters?

To address the situation, the government has what is called the earnings test. For 2023, you can earn up to $21,240 without it affecting your Social Security check if you're younger than full retirement age. But, for every $2 you earn past that amount, the Social Security Administration will withhold $1. The earnings test loosens in the year of your FRA; if you are reaching FRA in 2023, you can earn up to $56,520 before you run into the earnings test, and the government only withholds $1 for every $3 past that amount.

The month you reach FRA, you are no longer subject to any earnings withholding. For instance, if you are still working and will turn sixty-six on December 28, 2023, you would only have to worry about the earnings test until December, and then you can ignore it entirely. Keep in mind, the money the government withholds from your Social Security benefits while you are working before FRA will be tacked back onto your benefits check after FRA.[38]

One of the key elements of a financial plan is Social Security. Social Security was designed to be a supplement to your retirement income; it was never designed to be the most significant portion of your retirement income. However, people have begun to rely more on this government benefit through the years. Also, the Social Security system added many ancillary programs that have reduced resources.

Therefore it is more important now than ever that a person knows when they should turn on their Social Security. Consumers should know what happens with a benefit in case something happens in the event of a death or disability. There are several options available to a person. For example, the system is designed to give you more money per month the longer that you wait. However, there are some folks who desperately need the money as soon as it's available to them. When meeting with a financial advisor, Social Security should be one of the crucial conversations that take place within the planning process.

---

[38] Social Security Administration. "Receiving Benefits White Working" https://www.ssa.gov/benefits/retirement/planner/whileworking.html.

CHAPTER 6

401(k)s & IRAs

H ave you heard? Today's retirement is not your parents' retirement. You see, back in the day, it was pretty common to work for one company for the vast majority of your career and then retire with a gold watch and a pension.

The gold watch was a symbol of the quality time you had put in at that company, but the pension was more than a symbol. Instead, it was a guarantee—as solid as your employer—that they would repay your hard work with a certain amount of income in your old age. Did you see the caveat there? Your pension's guarantee was *as solid as your employer.* The problem was, what if your employer went under?

Companies that failed couldn't pay their retired employees' pensions, leading to financial challenges for many. Beginning in 1974 with Congress' passage of the Employee Retirement Income Security Act, federal legislation and regulations aimed at protecting retirees were everywhere. One piece of legislation included a relatively obscure section of the Internal Revenue Code, added in 1978. Section 401(k), to be specific.

IRC section 401, subsection k, created tax advantages for employer-sponsored financial products, even if the main contributor was the employee him or herself. Over the years, more employers took note, beginning an age of transition away from pensions and toward 401(k) plans. A 401(k) is a

73

retirement account with certain tax benefits and restrictions on the investments or other financial products inside of it.

Essentially, 401(k)s and their individual retirement account (IRA) counterparts are "wrappers" that provide tax benefits around assets; typically, the assets that compose IRAs and 401(k)s are mutual funds, stock and bond mixes, and money market accounts. However, IRA and 401(k) contents are becoming more diverse these days, with some companies offering different kinds of annuity options within their plans.

Where pensions are defined-*benefit* plans, 401(k)s and IRAs are defined-*contribution* plans. The one-word change outlines the basic difference. Pensions spell out what you can expect to receive from the plan but not necessarily how much money it will take to fund those benefits. With 401(k)s, an employer sets a standard for how much they will contribute (if any), and you can be certain of what you are contributing. Still, there is no outline for what you can expect to receive in return for those contributions.

Modern employment looks very different. A 2020 survey by the Bureau of Labor Statistics determined U.S. workers stayed with their employers a median of 4.1 years. Workers ages fifty-five to sixty-four had a little more staying power and were most likely to stay with their employer for about ten years.[39] Participation in 401(k) plans has steadily risen this century, totaling $7.3 trillion in assets in 2021 compared to $3.1 trillion in 2011. About 60 million active participants engaged in 401(k) plans in 2020.[40]

Over the last twenty or thirty years, corporate America has begun to reduce or even eliminate employee pension plans. They have relegated the responsibility of the employee's retirement back to the employee, by offering retirement tools such as 401(k)s. A 401(k) is nothing more than a bucket of

[39] Bureau of Labor Statistics. September 22, 2020. "Employee Tenure Summary." https://www.bls.gov/news.release/tenure.nro.htm
[40] Investment Company Institute. October 11, 2021. "Frequently Asked Questions About 401(k) Plan Research" https://www.ici.org/faqs/faq/401k/faqs_401k#

money that has yet to be taxed. An employee can choose to contribute a percentage of their income to the plan. Usually, the employer will match a piece of that income, enabling the worker to put it away for retirement.

One of the greatest benefits of a 401(k) is that you retain complete authority over how the funds get invested. However, one of the greatest risks inherent in 401(k) plans is that there is usually little education on how to invest the money. Even if employees gain insight into their investment options, will they save enough for retirement? Lastly, one of the other great risks is that this is a large bucket of money that has yet to be taxed. Unless a client knows how to manage the taxation of that account, it could create difficulties for them in retirement.

In years past, you went to work for a company for thirty or forty years. You did not have to put any money away for retirement because the company provided a long-term pension plan for both you and your spouse. I'm afraid those days are becoming part of a bygone era.

If there is anything to learn from this paradigm shift, it's that you must look out for yourself. Whether you have worked for a company for two years or twenty, you are still the one who has to look out for your own best interests. That holds doubly true when it comes to preparing for retirement. If you are one of the lucky ones who still has a pension, good for you. But for the rest of us, it is likely a 401(k)—or possibly one of its nonprofit- or government-sector counterparts, a 403(b) or 457 plan—is one of your biggest assets for retirement.

Some employers offer incentives to contribute to their company plans, like a company match. On that subject, I have one thing to say: *Do it!* Nothing in life is free, as they say, but a company match on your retirement funds is about as close to free money as it gets. If you can make the minimum to qualify for your company's match at all, go for it.

Now, it's likely, during our working years, we mostly "set and forget" our 401(k) funding. Because it is tax-advantaged, your employer is taking money from your paycheck—before taxes—and putting it into your plan for you. Maybe you got to pick a selection of investments, or maybe your company only offers one choice of investment in your 401(k). Either way, while you are gainfully employed, your most impactful decision may just be the decision to continue funding your plan in the first place. But, when you are ready to retire or move jobs, you have choices to make requiring a little more thought and care.

When you are ready to part ways with your job, you have a few options:

- Leave the money where it is
- Take the cash (and pay income taxes and perhaps a 10 percent additional federal tax if you are younger than age fifty-nine-and-one-half)
- Transfer the money to another employer plan (if the new plan allows)
- Roll the money over into a self-directed IRA

Now, these are just general options. You will have to decide, hopefully with the help of a financial professional, what's right for you. For instance, 401(k)s are typically pretty closely tied to the companies offering them, so when changing jobs, it may not always be possible to transfer a 401(k) to another 401(k). Leaving the money where it is may also be out of the question— some companies have direct cash payout or rollover policies once someone is no longer employed.

Also, remember what we mentioned earlier about how we change jobs more often these days? That means you likely have a 401(k) with your current company, but you may also have a string of retirement accounts trailing you from other jobs.

Due to the shift in our culture, it is not uncommon for people to have multiple jobs throughout their careers. Our grandfathers often went to work at one company and they stayed there for thirty or forty years, but that's not the case any longer. Due to technology, people have begun to migrate worldwide and can now work remotely from home. Many pick up and go to another company that matches their personalities better or provides more opportunities.

One of the risks we have seen is that when they leave a company, they sometimes leave their 401(k) at that company. Also, no one is usually managing those funds for their benefit. We try our very best to capture all of those assets and bring them back under one umbrella, so that clients can more effectively manage how much money they currently have and how much money they need for retirement. By regaining authority over managing those funds properly, the outcome often improves.

When it comes to your retirement income, it's important to be able to pull together *all* your assets, so you can examine what you have and where, and then decide what you will do with it.

Tax-Qualified, Tax-Preferred, Tax-Deferred ... Still TAXED

Financial media often cite IRAs and 401(k)s for their tax benefits. After all, with traditional plans, you put your money in, pre-tax, and it hopefully grows for years, even decades, untaxed. That's why these accounts are called "tax-qualified" or "tax-deferred" assets. They aren't *tax-free!* Rarely does Uncle Sam allow business to continue without receiving his piece of the pie, and your retirement assets are no different. If you didn't pay taxes on the front end, you will pay taxes on the money you withdraw from these accounts in retirement. Don't get me wrong: This isn't an inherently good or bad thing; it's just the way it is. It's important to understand, though, for the sake of planning ahead.

In retirement, many people assume they will be in a lower tax bracket. Are you planning to pare down your lifestyle in retirement? Perhaps you are, and perhaps you will have substantially less income in retirement. But many of my clients tell me they want to live life more or less the same as they always have. The money they would previously have spent on business attire or gas for their commute they now want to spend on hobbies and grandchildren. That's all fine, and for many of them, it is doable, but does it put them in a lower tax bracket? Probably not.

Keep in mind, IRAs, 401(k)s, and their alternatives have a few limitations because of their special tax status. For one thing, the IRS sets limits on your contributions to these retirement accounts. If you are contributing to a 401(k) or an equivalent nonprofit or government plan, your annual contribution limit is $22,500 (as of 2023). If you are fifty or older, the IRS allows additional contributions, called "catch-up contributions," of up to $7,500 on top of the regular limit of $22,500. For an IRA, the limit is $6,500, with a catch-up limit of an additional $1,000.[41] Beginning in 2024, catch-up contributions for individuals with income exceeding $145,000 must transfer into a Roth IRA.[42]

Because their tax advantages come from their intended use as retirement income, withdrawing funds from these accounts before you turn fifty-nine-and-one-half can carry stiff penalties. In addition to fees your investment management company might charge, you will have to pay income tax *and* a 10 percent federal tax penalty, with few exceptions.

The fifty-nine-and-one-half rule for retirement accounts is incredibly important to remember, especially when you're young. Younger workers are often tempted to cash out an IRA from a previous employer and then are surprised to find their checks missing 20 percent of the account value to income taxes, penalty taxes, and account fees.

Many millennials I see in my practice say, while they may be socking money away in their workplace retirement plan, it is often the *only* place they are saving. This could be problematic later because of the fifty-nine-and-one-half rule; what if you have an emergency? It is important to fund your retirement, but you need to have some liquid assets handy as emergency

[41] IRS.gov. December 8, 2022. "401(k) limit increases to $22,500 for 2023, IRA limit rises to $6,500" https://www.irs.gov/newsroom/401k-limit-increases-to-22500-for-2023-ira-limit-rises-to-6500
[42] Fidelity.com. 2023. "SECURE 2.0: Rethinking retirement savings" https://www.fidelity.com/learning-center/personal-finance/secure-act-2

funds. This can help you avoid breaking into your retirement accounts and incurring taxes and penalties because of the fifty-nine-and-one-half rule.

RMDs

Remember how we talked about the 401(k) or IRA being a "tax wrapper" for your funds? Well, eventually, Uncle Sam will want a bite of that candy bar. So, when you turn seventy-three, the government requires you withdraw a portion of your account, which the IRS calculates based on the size of your account and your estimated lifespan. This required minimum distribution, or RMD, is the government's insurance it will collect some taxes, at some point, from your earnings. Because you didn't pay taxes on the front end, you will now pay income taxes on whatever you withdraw, including your RMDs.

Let me reiterate something I pointed out in the Longevity chapter. Beginning at age seventy-three, you are required to withdraw a certain minimum amount every year from your 401(k) or IRA, or else you will face a tax penalty on any RMD monies you should have withdrawn but didn't—and that's on top of income tax. The SECURE Act 2.0 reduced the penalty to 25 percent (from 50 percent). Timely corrections also can reduce the penalty to 10 percent.[43]

Even after you begin RMDs, you can still also continue contributing to your 401(k) or IRAs if you are still employed, which can affect the whole discussion on RMDs and possible tax considerations. The SECURE Act 2.0 raised the RMD age to seventy-three from seventy-two. In addition, the latest legislation stipulates the RMD age will increase to seventy-five for those turning seventy-four after December 31, 2032.[44]

If you don't need income from your retirement accounts, RMDs can seem like more of a tax burden than an income boon.

---

[43] Jim Probasco. Investopedia.com. January 6, 2023. "SECURE 2.0 Act of 2022." https://www.investopedia.com/secure-2-0-definition-5225115
[44] Ibid.

While some people prefer to reinvest their RMDs, this comes with the possibility of additional taxation: You'll pay income taxes on your RMDs and then capital gains taxes on the growth of your investments. If you are legacy minded, there are other ways to use RMDs, many of which have tax benefits.

SECURE 2.0 Act provisions

In addition to changes imposed for RMD ages, Secure Act 2.0 also expanded access to retirement savings using different methods. Provisions in the legislation go into effect at different times, ranging from 2023-25.

- Beginning January 2, 2024, plan participants can access up to $1,000 (once a year) from retirement savings for emergency personal or family expenses without paying a 10 percent early withdrawal penalty.
- Beginning January 2, 2024, employees can establish a Roth emergency savings account of up to $2,500 per participant.
- Beginning January 2, 2024, domestic abuse survivors can withdraw the lesser of $10,000 or 50 percent of their retirement account without penalty.
- Beginning January 1, 2023, victims of a qualified, federally declared disaster can withdraw up to $22,000 from their retirement account without penalty.[45]

Permanent Life Insurance

One way to turn those pesky RMDs into a legacy is through permanent life insurance. Assuming you need the death benefit coverage and can qualify for it medically, if properly structured, these products can pass on a sizeable death benefit to your beneficiaries, tax-free, as part of your general legacy plan.

---

[45] Betterment.com. January 12, 2023. "SECURE Act 2.0: Signed into Law" https://www.betterment.com/work/resources/secure-act-2

ILIT

Another way to use RMDs toward your legacy is to work with an estate planning attorney to create an irrevocable life insurance trust (ILIT). This is basically a permanent life insurance policy placed within a trust. Because the trust is irrevocable, you would relinquish control of it, but, unlike with just a permanent life insurance policy, your death benefit won't count toward your taxable estate.

Annuities

Because annuities can be tax-deferred, using all or a portion of your RMDs to fund an annuity contract can be one way to further delay taxation while guaranteeing your income payments (either to you or your loved ones) later. (Assuming you don't need the RMD income during your retirement.)

Qualified Charitable Distributions

If you are charity-minded, you may use your RMDs toward a charitable organization instead of using them for income. You must do this directly from your retirement account (you can't take the RMD check and *then* pay the charity) for your withdrawals to be qualified charitable distributions (QCDs), but this is one way of realizing some of the benefits of a charitable legacy during your own lifetime. You will not need to pay taxes on your QCDs, and they won't count toward your annual charitable tax deduction limit, plus you'll be able to see how the organization you are supporting uses your donations. You should consult a financial professional on how to correctly make a QCD, particularly since the SECURE Act has implemented a few regulations on this point.[46]

Tax consequences of 401(k)s and IRAs can be considerable unless consumers plan properly. The government knows that

---

[46] Bob Carlson. Forbes. January 28, 2020. "More Questions And Answers About The SECURE Act."
https://www.forbes.com/sites/bobcarlson/2020/01/28/more-questions-and-answers-about-the-secure-act/#113d49564869

your dollars have yet to be taxed and has set up a special set of rules to assure that it gets a piece of the pie. At age fifty-nine-and-one-half, a person can reach into their IRAs and withdraw funds without penalty. While you can never avoid the taxes you must eventually pay on the IRA, you can avoid the premature penalties that the IRS would have established upon that account when you were younger than fifty-nine-and-one-half.

At age seventy-three, unless the money is gone, you are required to begin to withdraw a percentage of the money annually because the government wants to make sure it is taxing those dollars. The problem with that situation is that the government dictates how much money it gets out of your 401(k) and your IRA. However, with some strategic planning, you can retain some control over how much to give up to taxation. By doing some tax planning on the account, potentially moving some or all of those dollars over to a Roth IRA through conversions could prove advantageous in the future.

Suppose the government is your partner in your 401(k) because of the taxes it collects. Altering the tax burden can help determine just how big a role the government can play as your "partner."

Roth IRA

Since the Taxpayer Relief Act of 1997, there has been a different kind of retirement account, or "tax wrapper," available to the public: the Roth. Roth IRAs and Roth 401(k)s each differ from their traditional counterparts in one big way: You pay your taxes on the front end. This means, once your post-tax money is in the Roth account, as long as you follow the rules and limitations of that account, your distributions are truly tax-free. You won't pay income tax when you take withdrawals, so, in turn, you don't have to worry about RMDs. However, Roth accounts have the same limitations as traditional 401(k)s and IRAs when it comes to withdrawing money before age fifty-nine-and-one-half, with the added stipulation that the account

210 RETIREMENT BLUEPRINT | 83

must have been open for at least five years in order for the accountholder to make withdrawals.

A Roth conversion involves taking dollars from an IRA or a 401(k) that have yet to be taxed, causing a taxable situation by moving them from that particular bucket of money to a Roth IRA. When that conversion takes place, it causes a taxable event. While the initial tax consequence can be significant, funds withdrawn from a Roth IRA do not incur a tax after you turn fifty-nine-and-one-half and the account has been open for at least five years. In addition, if you decide not to spend all of your money and you were to leave it to your beneficiaries, they will not incur taxes from funds in a Roth IRA.

One of the things we have seen is that when a person passes away, they usually do so when their children are in their greatest earnings years. If you leave them an IRA or a 401(k), the tax burden could be detrimental to them. However, if they inherit your Roth, they get to do so tax-free. This could have a nice impact on the legacy one leaves.

Taking Charge

As mentioned earlier, the 401(k) and IRA have largely replaced pensions, but they aren't an equal trade.

Pensions are employer-funded; the money feeding into them is money that wouldn't ever show up on your pay stub. Because 401(k)s are self-funded, you must actively and consciously save. This distinction has made a difference when it comes to funding retirement. Fidelity Investments published a story detailing that the average 401(k) balance for a person age fifty-five to sixty-four is $189,800, but the median likely tells the full story. The median 401(k) balance for a person age fifty-five to sixty-four is $56,450. Those figures reflect Fidelity accounts from the third quarter of 2022.[47]

---

[47] Arielle O'Shea. Nerd Wallet. December 22, 2022. "The Average 401(k) Balance by Age" https://www.nerdwallet.com/article/investing/the-average-401k-balance-by-age

There can be many reasons why people underfund their retirement plans, like being overwhelmed by the investment choices or taking withdrawals from IRAs when they leave an employer, but the reason at the top of the list is this: People simply aren't participating to begin with.

So, whether you use a 401(k) with an employer or an IRA alternative with a private company, separate from your workplace, the most important retirement savings decision you can make is to sock away your money somewhere in the first place.

Investing involves risk, including the potential loss of principal. No investment strategy can guarantee a profit or protect against loss in periods of declining values. Any references to protection benefits or guaranteed/lifetime income streams refer only to fixed insurance products, not securities or investment products. Insurance and annuity product guarantees are backed by the financial strength and claims-paying ability of the issuing insurance company.

Insurance products are offered through the insurance business 210 Financial. 210 Financial is also an Investment Advisory practice that offers products and services through AE Wealth Management, LLC (AEWM), a Registered Investment Advisor. AEWM does not offer insurance products. The insurance products offered by 210 Financial are not subject to Investment Advisor requirements.

Please remember that converting an employer plan account to a Roth IRA is a taxable event. Increased taxable income from the Roth IRA conversion may have several consequences Be sure to consult with a qualified tax advisor before making any decisions regarding your IRA.

Neither the firm nor its agents or representatives may give tax or legal advice. Individuals should consult with a qualified professional for guidance before making any purchasing decisions.

CHAPTER 7

Annuities

In my practice, I offer my clients a variety of products—from securities to insurance—all designed to help them reach their financial goals. You may be wondering: Why single out a single product in this book?

Well, while most of my clients have a pretty good understanding of business and finance, I sometimes find those who have the impression there must be magic involved. Some people assume there is a magic finance wand we can wave to change years' worth of savings into a strategy for retirement income. But it's not as easy as a goose laying golden eggs or the Fairy Godmother turning a pumpkin into a coach!

Finances aren't magic; it takes lots of hard work and, typically, several financial products and strategies to pull together a complete retirement plan. Of all the financial products I work with, it seems people find none more mysterious than annuities. And, if I may say, even some of those who recognize the word "annuity" have a limited understanding of the product. So, in the interest of demystifying annuities, let me tell you a little about what an annuity is.

In general, insurance is a financial hedge against risk. Car owners buy auto insurance to protect their finances in case they injure someone or someone injures them. Homeowners have house insurance to protect their finances in case of a fire, flood, or another disaster. People have life insurance to protect their finances in case of untimely death. Almost juxtaposed to life insurance, people have annuities in case of a long life; annuities can give you financial protection by providing consistent and reliable income payments.

The basic premise of an annuity is you, the annuitant, pay an insurance company some amount in exchange for their contractual guarantee they will pay you income for a certain time period. How that company pays you, for how long, and how much they offer are all determined by the annuity contract you enter into with the insurance company.

How You Get Paid

There are two ways for an annuity contract to provide income: The first is through what is called annuitization, and the second is through the use of income riders. We'll get into income riders in a bit, but let's talk about annuitization. That nice, long word is, in my opinion, one reason annuities have a reputation for mystery and misinformation.

Annuitization

When someone "annuitizes" a contract, it is the point where he or she turns on the income stream. Once a contract has been annuitized, there is no going back. With annuities, if the policyholder lives longer than the insurance company planned, the insurance company is still obligated to pay him or her, even if the payments end up being way more than the contract's actual value. If, however, the policyholder dies an untimely death, depending on the contract type, the insurance company may keep anything left of the money that funded the annuity—nothing would be paid out to the contract holder's survivors. You see where that could make some people balk? Now, modern annuities rarely rely on annuitization for the income portion of the contract, and instead have so many bells and whistles that the old concept of annuitization seems outdated, but because this is still an option, it's important to at least understand the basic concept.

Riders

Speaking of bells and whistles, let's talk about riders. Modern annuities have a lot of different options these days, many in the form of riders you can add to your contract for a fee—usually about 1 percent of the contract value per year. Each rider has its particulars, and the types of riders available will vary by the type of annuity contract purchased, but I'll just briefly outline some of these little extras:

- Lifetime income rider: Contract guarantees you an enhanced or flexible income for life
- Death benefit rider: Contract pays an enhanced death benefit to your beneficiaries even if you have annuitized
- Return of premium rider: Guarantees you (or your beneficiaries) will at least receive back the premium value of the annuity
- Long-term care rider: Provides a certain amount, sometimes as much as twice the normal income benefit amount for a period of time to help pay for long-term care if the contract holder is moved to a nursing home or assisted living situation

This isn't an extensive look, and usually the riders have fancier names based on the issuing company, like "Lorem Ipsum Insurance Company Income Preferred Bonus Fixed Index Annuity rider," but I just wanted to show you what some of the general options are in layperson's terms.

Types of Annuities

Annuities break down into four basic types: immediate, variable, fixed, and fixed index.

Immediate

Immediate annuities primarily rely on annuitization to provide income—you give the insurance company a lump sum up front, and your payments begin immediately. Once you begin receiving income payments, the transaction is irreversible, and you no longer have access to your money in a lump sum. When you die, any remaining contract value is typically forfeited to the insurance company.

All other annuity contract types are "deferred" contracts, meaning you fund your policy as a lump sum or over a period of years and you give it the opportunity to grow over time—sometimes years, sometimes decades.

Variable

A variable annuity is an insurance contract as well as an investment. It's sold by insurance companies, but only through someone who is registered to sell investment products. With a variable annuity contract, the insurance company invests your premiums in subaccounts that are tied to the stock market. This makes it a bit different from the other annuity contract types because it is the only contract where your money is subject to losses because of market declines. Your contract value has a greater opportunity to grow, but it also stands to lose. Additionally, your contract's value will be subject to the underlying investment's fees and limitations—including capital gains taxes, management fees, etc. Once it is time for you to receive income from the contract, the insurance company will pay you a certain income, locked in at whatever your contract's value was.

Fixed

A traditional fixed annuity is pretty straightforward. You purchase a contract with a guaranteed interest rate and, when you are ready, the insurance company will make regular income payments to you at whatever payout rate your contract guarantees. Those payments will continue for the rest of your life and, if you choose, for the remainder of your spouse's life.

Fixed annuities don't typically offer significant upside potential, but many people like them for their guarantees (after all, if your Aunt May lives to be ninety-five, knowing she has a paycheck later in life can be her mental and financial safety net), as well as for their predictability. Unlike variable annuities, which are subject to market risk and might be up one year and down the next, you can easily calculate the value of your fixed annuity over your lifetime.

Fixed Index

To recap, variable annuities take on more risk to offer more possibilities to grow. Fixed annuities have less potential growth, but they protect your principal. In the last couple of decades, many insurance companies have retooled their product line to offer fixed index annuities, which are sort of midway between variable and fixed annuities on that risk/reward spectrum. Fixed index annuities offer greater growth potential than traditional fixed annuities but less than variable annuities. Like traditional fixed annuities, however, fixed index annuities are protected from downside market losses.

Fixed index annuities earn interest that is tied to an external market index, meaning that, instead of your contract value growing at a set interest rate like a traditional fixed annuity, it has the potential to grow within a range. Your contract's value is credited interest based on the performance of an external market index like the S&P 500 while never being invested in the market itself. You can't invest in the S&P 500 directly, but each year, your annuity as the potential to earn interest based on the chosen index's performance, subject to limits set by the company such as caps, spreads and participation rates. For instance, if your contract caps your interest at 5 percent, then in a year that the S&P 500 gains 3 percent, your annuity value increases 3 percent. If the S&P 500 gains 35 percent, your annuity value gets a 5 percent interest bump. But since your money isn't actually invested in the market with a fixed index annuity, if the market nosedives (such as happened during 2000, 2008 and 2020, anyone?) you won't see any increase in your contract value. Conversely, there will also be no decrease in your contract value—no matter how badly the market performed, as long as you follow the terms of the contract, you won't lose any of the interest you were credited in previous years.

So, what if the S&P 500 shows a market loss of 30 percent? Your contract value isn't going anywhere (unless you purchased an optional rider—this charge will still come out of your annuity value each year). For those who are more interested in protection than growth potential, fixed index annuities can be an attractive option because, when the stock market has a long period of positive performance, a fixed index annuity can enjoy conservative growth. And, during stretches where the stock market is erratic and stock values across the board take significant losses? Fixed index annuities won't lose anything due to the stock market volatility.

A fixed index annuity is a tool that is widely misunderstood. Given the right set of instructions, however, it could be a tool that is beneficial and cost-effective. FIAs assure no losses due to market corrections. They can pay a guaranteed income stream for the rest of your life or even the lives of you and your spouse. They can provide many other benefits such as annual locking of credited interest each year. An FIA can be a great tool if used properly. During the market corrections of 2001 or 2008, or even the COVID-19 correction of 2020, some clients experienced great benefits from these types of tools. They do not allow a person's money to decline due to market corrections.

This can be a significant relief to someone who turns on the news and sees that the market is highly volatile like it was during the COVID correction. Yet they know the money in their annuity has not gone down because it was allocated to a fixed index annuity.

Other Things to Know About Annuities

We just talked about the four kinds of annuity contracts available, but all of them have some commonalities as annuities.

For all annuities, the contractual guarantees are only as strong as the insurance company that sells the product, which makes it important to thoroughly check the credit ratings of any company whose products you are considering.

Annuities are tax-deferred, meaning you don't have to pay taxes on interest earnings each year as the contract value grows. Instead, you will pay ordinary income taxes on your withdrawals. These are meant to be long-term products, so, like other tax-deferred or tax-advantaged products, if you begin taking withdrawals from your contract before age fifty-nine-and-one-half, you may also have to pay a 10 percent federal tax penalty. Also, while annuities are generally considered illiquid, most contracts allow you to withdraw up to 10 percent of your contract value every year. Withdraw any more, however, and you could incur additional surrender penalties.

Keep in mind, your withdrawals will deplete the accumulated cash value, death benefit, and, possibly, the rider values of your contract.

Just picture a day when the markets are volatile, yet you can be reassured that the money in your annuity is protected from loss. This can happen with an FIA because these instruments do not allow for market-corrected negative returns.

Also, picture a day when the market goes up, and you may be able to benefit by receiving—and locking in—interest credits, which are usually calculated annually.Then, if the market declines after that date, you still get to keep those credits.

Annuities aren't for everyone, but it's important to understand them before saying "yea" or "nay" on whether they fit into your plan; otherwise, you're not operating with complete information, wouldn't you agree? Regardless, you should talk to a financial professional who can help you understand annuities, help you dissect your particular financial needs, and help show you whether an annuity is appropriate for your retirement income plan.

CHAPTER 8

Estate & Legacy

I n my practice, I devote a significant portion of my time to matters of estates. That doesn't mean drawing up wills or trusts or putting together powers of attorney or anything like that. After all, I'm not an estate planning attorney. But I am a financial professional, and what part of the "estate" isn't affected by money matters?

I've included this chapter because I have seen many people do estate planning wrong. Clients, or clients' families, have come in after experiencing a death in the family and have found themselves in the middle of probate, high taxes, or a discovery of something unforeseen (often long-term care) draining the estate.

I have also seen people do estate planning right: clients or families who visit my office to talk about legacies and how to make them last and adult children who have room to grieve without an added burden of unintended costs, without stress from a family ruptured because of inadequate planning.

I'll share some of these stories here. However, I'm not going to give you specific advice, since everyone's situation is unique. I only want to give you some things to think about and to underscore the importance of planning ahead.

One of the most important elements of a strong financial plan hinges on constructing legal documents. At 210 Financial, we are not attorneys. But we advise our clients to meet with a qualified estate planning attorney, and make a strong plan to help ensure their final documents are in place. Those final documents will typically include a will and powers of attorney. These documents help ensure that your assets transfer to the people you want them to transfer to in a tax-efficient and seamless way.

Powers of attorney are documents that will dictate who gets to help you make decisions should you become disabled in the future. These loved ones will speak to doctors, make financial decisions, and even buy or sell a home if you need someone to handle such matters. The lack of such documents can create a void in someone's retirement plan. We will ask clients if they have a will in place. Sometimes, people will look at each other, shrug and say, "I think we do." Or they say,"We always wanted to do that." Still, they haven't actually done it. It's one of those ironic things in financial planning, where we all know we're going to die; we just don't want to talk about it. A good financial planner's job is to make sure that legal documentation is a piece of the puzzle that gets put in place.

You Can't Take It With You

When it comes to legacy and estate planning, the most important thing is to *do it*. I have heard people from clients to celebrities (rap artist Snoop Dogg comes to mind) say they aren't interested in what happens to their assets when they die because they'll be dead. That's certainly one way to look at it. But I think that's a very selfish way to go about things—we all have people and causes we care about, and those who care about us. Even if the people we love don't *need* what we leave behind, they can still be fined or legally tied up in the probate process or burial costs if we don't plan for those. And that's not even considering what happens if you become incapacitated at some point while you are still alive. Having a plan in place can greatly reduce the stress of those responsibilities on your loved ones; it's just a loving thing to do.

Documents

There are a few documents that lay the groundwork of legacy planning. You've probably heard of all or most of them, but I'd like to review what they are and how people commonly use them. These are all things you should talk about with an estate planning attorney to establish your legacy.

Powers of Attorney

A power of attorney, or POA, is a document giving someone the authority to act on your behalf and in your best interests. These come in handy in situations where you cannot be present (think a vacation where you get stuck in Canada) or, for durable powers of attorney, even when you are incapacitated (think in a coma or coping with dementia).

It is important to have powers of attorney in place and to appoint someone you trust to act on your behalf in these matters. Have you ever heard of someone who was incapacitated after a car accident, whether from head trauma or being in a coma for weeks—sometimes months? Do you think their bills stopped coming due during that time? I like my phone company and my bank, but neither one is about to put a moratorium on sending me bills, particularly not for an extended or interminable period. A power of attorney would have the authority to pay your mortgage or cancel your cable while you are unable.

You can have multiple POAs and require them to act jointly.
What this looks like: Do you think two heads are better than one? One man, Chris, significantly relied on his two sons' opinions for both his business and personal matters. He appointed both sons as joint POA, requiring both their signoffs for his medical and financial matters.

You can have multiple POAs who can act independently.

What this looks like: Irene had three children with whom she routinely stayed. They lived in different areas of the country, which she thought was an advantage; one month she might be hiking out West, the next she could enjoy the newest off-Broadway production, and the next she could soak up some Southern sun. She named her three children as independently authorized POAs, so, if something happened, no matter where she was, the child closest could step in to act on her behalf.

You can have POAs who have different responsibilities.

What this looks like: Although Luke's friend Claire, a nurse, was his go-to and POA for health-related issues, financial matters usually made her nervous, so he appointed his good neighbor, Matt, as his POA in all of his financial and legal matters.

In addition to POAs, it may be helpful to have an advanced medical directive. This is a document where you have pre-decided what choices you would make about different health scenarios. An advanced medical directive can help ease the burden for your medical POA and loved ones, particularly when it comes to end-of-life care.

We have all heard of the famous person dying without a will and then their assets get tied up in court for years and years. Even though we may not have as much money or as much notoriety as these people, the consequences of not having a will could create hardship for our loved ones.

Our children, grandchildren and family legacy can benefit from the proper implementation of wills and powers of attorney that verify our wishes. I would suggest that it is probably your last desire not to have your family fighting over assets after you pass. An easy way to help eliminate this type of frustration within a family is to ensure that your end-of-life documents are in place. Again, that would likely include a will and powers of attorney.

Wills

Perhaps the most basic document of legacy planning, a will is a legal document wherein you outline your wishes for your estate. When it comes to your estate after your death, having a will is the foundation of your legacy. Without one, your loved ones are left behind, guessing what you would have wanted, and the court will likely split your assets according to the state's defaults. Maybe that's exactly what you wanted, as far as anyone knows, right? Because even if you told your nephew he could have your car he's been driving, if it's not in writing, it still might go to the brother, sister, son, or daughter to whom you aren't speaking.

However, it may not be enough just to have a will. Even with a will, your assets will be subject to probate. Probate is what we call the state's process for determining a will's validity. A judge will go through your will to question if it conflicts with state law, if it is the most up-to-date document, if you were mentally competent at the time it was in order, etc. For some, this is a quick, easily-resolved process. For others, particularly if someone steps forward to contest the will, it may take years to settle, all the while subjecting the assets to court costs and attorney's fees.

One other undesirable piece of the probate process is that it is a public process. That means anyone can go to the courthouse, ask for copies of the case, and discover your assets. They can also see who is slated to receive what and who is disputing.

It's also important to remember beneficiary lines trump wills. So, that large life insurance policy? What if, when you bought it fifteen years ago, you wrote your ex-husband's name on the beneficiary line? Even if you stipulate otherwise in your will, the company that holds your policy will pay out to your ex-spouse. Or, how about the thousands of dollars in your IRA you dedicated to the children thirty years ago, but one of your children was killed in a car accident, leaving his wife and two toddlers behind? That IRA is going to transfer to your remaining children, with nothing for your daughter-in-law and grandchildren.

That may paint a grim portrait, but I can't underscore enough the importance of working with a skilled estate planning attorney to keep your will and beneficiary lines up to date as your life changes, for the sake of your loved ones.

One of the final pieces of guidance I can give you on your estate plan is to ensure that your beneficiaries align with your values. This verification process is especially important if you have been in multiple marriages or if you have children from multiple marriages. Just make sure that your beneficiary arrangements, your wills, and your powers of attorney are in line with each other, and they do what you want them to do so there are no issues after you pass.

We have often seen that emotions can take over when a family deals with money and possessions, contributing to irrational decisions. Such decisions often strain relationships. You can take precautions to help prevent this from happening within your family.

Trusts

Another piece of legacy planning to consider is the trust.

A trust is set up through an attorney and allows a third party, or trustee, to hold your assets and determine how they will pass to your beneficiaries. Many people are skeptical of trusts because they assume trusts are only appropriate for the fabulously wealthy.

However, a simple trust may only cost $1,000 to $2,500 in attorney's fees and can avoid both the expense and publicity of probate, provide a more immediate transfer of wealth, avoid some taxes, and provide you greater control over your legacy.[48]

For instance, if you want to set aside some funds for a grandchild's college education, you can make it a requirement

---

[48] Regan Rondinelli-Haberek. LegalZoom. "What is the Average Cost to Prepare a Living Trust?" https://info.legalzoom.com/average-cost-prepare-living-trust-26932.html

he or she enrolls in classes before your trust will dispense any funds. Like a will, beneficiary lines will override your trust conditions, so you must still keep insurance policies and other assets up to date.

Like any financial or legal consideration, there are many options these days beyond the simple "yes or no" question of whether to have a trust. For one thing, you will need to consider if you want your trust to be revocable (you can change the terms while you are alive) or irrevocable (can't be changed; you are no longer the "owner" of the contents). A brief note here about irrevocable trusts: Although they have significant and greater tax benefits, they are still subject to a Medicaid look-back period. If you transfer your assets into an irrevocable trust to shelter them from a Medicaid spend-down, you will be ineligible for Medicaid coverage of long-term care for five years. Yet, an irrevocable trust can avoid both probate and estate taxes and can even protect assets from legal judgments against you.

Another thing to remember when it comes to trusts, in general, is, even if you have set up a trust, you must remember to fund it. In our company's twenty-plus years in operation, I've had numerous clients come to me, assuming they have protected their assets with a trust. When we talk about taxes and other pieces of their legacy, it turns out they never retitled any assets or changed any paperwork on the assets they wanted in the trust. So, please remember, a trust is just a bunch of fancy legal papers if you haven't followed through on retitling your assets.

Taxes

Although charitable contributions, trusts, and other tax-efficient strategies can reduce your tax bill, it's unlikely your estate will be passed on entirely tax-free. Yet, when it comes to building a legacy that can last for generations, taxes can be one of the heaviest drains on the impact of your hard work.

For 2020, the federal estate exemption was $11.58 million per individual and $23.16 million for a married couple, with estates facing up to a 40 percent tax rate after that. In 2022, those limits increased to $12.06 million for individuals and $24.12 million for married couples, with the 40 percent top level gift and estate tax remaining the same. Currently, the new estate limits are set to increase with inflation until January 1, 2026, when they will "sunset" back to the inflation-adjusted 2017 limits.[49] And that's not taking into account the various state regulations and taxes regarding estate and inheritance transfers.

Another tax concern "frequent flyer": retirement accounts.

Your IRA or 401(k) can be a source of tax issues when you pass away. For one thing, taking funds from a sizeable account can trigger a large tax bill. However, if you leave the assets in the account, there are still required minimum distributions (RMDs), which will take effect even after you die. If you pass the account to your spouse, he or she can keep taking your RMDs as is, or your spouse can retitle the account in his or her name and receive RMDs based on his or her life expectancy. Remember, if you don't take your RMDs, the IRS will take up to 25 percent of your required distribution (10 percent if corrections are made in a timely fashion), You will still have to pay income taxes whenever you withdraw that money. Provisions in the original SECURE Act, anyone who inherits your IRA, with few exceptions (your spouse, a beneficiary less than ten years younger, or a disabled adult child, to name a few), will need to empty the account within ten years of your death.

Also—and this is a pretty big also—check with an attorney if you are considering putting your IRA or 401(k) in a trust. An improperly titled beneficiary form for the IRA could mean the difference of thousands of dollars in taxes. This is just one more

---

[49] Laura Sanders, Richard Rubin. The Wall Street Journal. March 10, 2022. "Estate and Gift Taxes 2021-2022: "What's New This Year and What You Need to Know." https://www.wsj.com/articles/estate-and-gift-taxes-what-to-know-2021-2022-11646426764

reason to work with a financial professional, one who can strategically partner with an estate planning attorney to diligently check your decisions.

CHAPTER 9

Women Retire Too

I help men, women, and families from all walks of life on their journey to and through retirement. Yet, I want to address the female demographic specifically. Why? To be perfectly blunt, women are more likely to deal with poverty than men when they reach retirement. In 2020, the overall poverty rate for women (16.4 percent) exceeded the rate for men (15.7 percent).[50]

The topics, products, and strategies I cover elsewhere in this book are meant to help address retirement concerns for men *and* women, but the dire statistic above is a reminder that much of traditional planning is geared toward men. Male careers, male lifespans, male health care. The bottom line is women's career paths often look much different than men's, so why would their retirement planning look the same?

Women often embrace different roles and values than men as workers, wives, mothers, and daughters. They are more apt to take on roles as caretakers. They often plan for events, worry about loved ones, tend to details, and think about the future. Also, they often want everything to be just right, and they want to be right themselves. It could be you've seen the following affixed to a decorative sign, refrigerator magnet, or T-shirt: "If

I agreed with you, we'd both be wrong." The barb features a picture of a woman speaking to a man.

If these characteristics I listed about women are accurate, shouldn't they deserve special considerations from financial professionals? The case can be made, particularly since 69 percent of men in the U.S. age 65 and older happen to be married, compared to 47 percent of women in that age classification.[51] Single women don't have the opportunity to capitalize on the resource pooling and potential economies of scale accompanying a marriage or partnership.

We believe that a woman should be one of, if not the most important, person in the financial planning process simply because, statistically, they're going to outlive the man in the relationship.

There were times in our country when women assumed a different role that sometimes precluded them from getting involved in financial matters. However, today we believe that women should have just as strong, if not a stronger say so, with any financial planning process due to the fact that they could easily outlive the husband in their relationship. Some crucial factors could take place if one of them passes away such as their income tax now goes to filing at a single rate. Sometimes, this places the surviving spouse into a higher tax bracket.Questions need to be answered in the planning stages. Among them: What happens to a husband's pension, or what happens to his Social Security benefit should his wife be the one left a widow after he passes away?

Be Informed

It's a familiar scene in many financial offices across the country: A woman comes into an appointment carrying a sack full of unopened envelopes. Often through tears, she sits across the

---

[51] Administration for Community Living. November 30, 2022. "Profile of Older Americans." https://acl.gov/aging-and-disability-in-america/data-and-research/profile-older-americans

desk from a financial professional and apologizes her way through a conversation about what financial products she owns and where her income is coming from. She is recently widowed and was sure her spouse was taking care of the finances, but now she doesn't know where all their assets are kept, and her confidence in her financial outlook has wavered after walking through funeral expenses and realizing she's down to one income.

Often, she may be financially "okay." Yet, the uncertainty can be wearying, particularly when the family is already reeling from a loss. While this scenario sometimes plays out with men, in my experience, it's more likely to be a woman in that chair across from my desk, probably, in part, because of Western traditions about money management being "a guy thing." But it doesn't have to be this way. This all-too-common scenario can be wiped away with just a little preparation.

Talk to Your Spouse/ Work with a Financial Professional

While there are many factors affecting women's financial preparation for and situation in retirement, I cannot emphasize enough that the decision to be informed, to be a part of the conversation, and to be aware of what is going on with your finances is absolutely paramount to a confident retirement. With all the couples I've seen, there is almost always an "alpha" when it comes to finances. It isn't always men—for many of my coupled clients, the wife is the alpha who keeps the books and budgets and knows where all of the family's assets are, down to the penny—yet, statistically, among baby boomers it is usually a man who runs the books. But, as time goes on, it looks like the ratio of male to female financial alphas is evening out. According to a Gallup study, women are equally as likely to take the lead on finances as men, with 37 percent of U.S. households showing women primarily paying the bills. Half of households also say decisions about savings and investments are shared equally.[52] Whether that's the way your household works or not, there isn't anything wrong with who does what.

The breakdown happens when there is a lack of communication, when no one other than the financial alpha knows how much the family has and where. In the end, it doesn't matter who handles the money; it's about all parties being informed of what's going on financially.

There are a lot of ways to open the conversation about money. One woman started a conversation with her husband, the financial alpha, by sitting down and saying, "Teach me how to be a widow." Perhaps that sounds grim, but it was to the point, and it spurred what she said was a very fruitful conversation. Couples sometimes have their first real conversation about money, assets, and their retirement income approach, in our office. The important thing about having these conversations isn't where, it's when . . . and the best "when" is as soon as possible.

A woman once commented to me that to get this conversation rolling, she asked her husband "to teach her how to be a widow." They spent a day, just one part of an otherwise dull weekend, going through everything she might need to know. They spent the better part of two decades together after that. When he died, and she was widowed, she said the "widowhood" talk had made a huge difference. She knew who to call to talk through their retirement plan and where to call for the insurance policy.

She said the fruit of the weekend exercise they engaged in some twenty years earlier couldn't have been more apparent than when she ultimately accompanied a recently widowed friend of hers to a financial appointment. Her friend was emotional the whole time, afraid she would run out of money any day. The financial professional ultimately showed the friend that she was financially in good shape, but not before the

[52] Megan Brenan. Gallup. January 29, 2020. "Women Still Handle Main Household Tasks in U.S." https://news.gallup.com/poll/283979/women-handle-main-household-tasks.aspx

friend had already spent months worried that each check would exhaust her bank account. That's no way to live after losing a loved one. It was preventable had her deceased spouse and financial professional included her in a conversation about "widowhood."

Spouse-Specific Options

One area where it might be especially important to be on the same page between spouses is when it comes to financial products or services that have spousal options. A few that come to mind are pensions and Social Security, although life insurance and annuity policies also have the potential to affect both spouses.

With pensions, taking the worker's life-only option is somewhat attractive—after all, the monthly payment is bigger. However, you and your spouse should discuss your options. When we're talking about both of you, as opposed to just one lifespan, there is an increased likelihood at least one of you will live a long, long time. This means the monthly payout will be less, but it also ensures that, no matter which spouse outlives the other, no one will have to suffer the loss of a needed pension paycheck in his or her later retirement years.

While we covered Social Security options in a different chapter, I think some of the spousal information bears repeating. Particularly, if you worked exclusively inside the home for a significant number of years, you may want to talk about taking your Social Security benefits based on your spouse's work history. After all, Social Security is based on your thirty-five highest-earning years.

Things to remember about the spousal benefits:[53]

- Your benefit will be calculated as a percentage (up to 50 percent) of your spouse's earned monthly benefit at his or her full retirement age, or FRA.

---

[53] Social Security Administration. "Retirement Planner: Benefits For You As A Spouse." https://www.ssa.gov/planners/retire/applying6.html

- For you to begin receiving a spousal benefit, your spouse must have already filed for his or her own benefits and you must be at least sixty-two.
- You can qualify for a full half of your spouse's benefits if you wait until you reach FRA to file.
- Beginning your benefits earlier than your FRA will reduce your monthly check but waiting to file until after FRA will not increase your benefits.

For divorcees:[54]

- You may qualify for an ex-spousal benefit if . . .
  a. You were married for a decade or more
  b. *and* you are at least sixty-two
  c. *and* you have been divorced for at least two years
  d. *and* you are currently unmarried
  e. *and* your ex-spouse is sixty-two (qualifies to begin taking Social Security)
- Your ex-spouse does not need to have filed for you to file on his or her benefit.
- Similar to spousal benefits, you can qualify for up to half of your ex-spouse's benefits if you wait to file until your FRA.
- If your ex-spouse dies, you may file to receive a widow/widower benefit on his or her Social Security record as long as you are at least age sixty and fulfill all the other requirements on the preceding alphabetized list.
  a. This will not affect the benefits of your ex-spouse's current spouse

For widow's (or widower's, for that matter) benefits:[55]

---

54 Social Security Administration. "Retirement Planner: If You Are Divorced." https://www.ssa.gov/planners/retire/divspouse.html
55 Social Security Administration. "Survivors Planner: If You Are The Worker's Widow Or Widower." https://www.ssa.gov/planners/survivors/ifyou.html#h2

- You may qualify to receive as much as your deceased spouse would have received if . . .
  a. You were married for at least nine months before his or her death
  b. **or** you would qualify for a divorced spousal benefit
  c. **and** you are at least sixty
  d. **and** you did not/have not remarried before age sixty
- You may earn delayed credits on your spouse's benefit *if* your spouse hadn't already filed for benefits when he or she died.
- Other rules may apply to you if you are disabled or are caring for a deceased spouse's dependent or disabled child.

Longevity

On average, women live longer than men. Most stats put average female longevity at about two years more than men. But averages are tricky things. An April 2022 report by the World Economic Forum listed the eight oldest people in the world to all be women. They ranged in age from 118 years old to 114 and included two Americans.[56]

On one hand, this is a Brandi Chastain moment. You know, when the American soccer icon shed her jersey to celebrate a game-winning penalty kick to win the World Cup. Seriously, how fabulous are women? They tend to be meticulous, resolute, and perseverant. On the other hand, the trend for women to live longer presents longstanding financial ramifications.

At our firm, we host an annual Valentine's Day banquet for all clients who are widows. We have welcomed more than

---

[56] Martin Armstrong. World Economic Forum. April 29, 2022. "How old are the world's oldest people?" https://www.weforum.org/agenda/2022/04/the-oldest-people-in-the-world/

seventy-five ladies to this event. What's interesting is it's not just for ladies. It's for anyone who has been widowed. Yet to my astonishment, men rarely attend the event. This speaks volumes to the fact that ladies usually outlive their husbands. Therefore, they should know as much or more about their financial situation as the husband does.

Simply Needing More Money in Retirement

Living longer in retirement means needing more money, period. Barring a huge lottery win or some crazy stock market action, the date you retire is likely the point at which you have the most money you will ever have. Not to put too grim a spin on it, but the problem with longevity is, the further you get away from that date, the further your dollars have to stretch. If you planned to live to a nice eighty-something but live to a nice one-hundred-something, that is *two decades* you will need to account for, monetarily.

To put this in perspective, let's say you like to drink coffee as an everyday splurge. Not accounting for inflation or leap years, a $2.50 cup-a-day habit is $18,250 over a two-decade span. Now, think of all the things you like to do that cost money. Add those up for twenty years of unanticipated costs. I think you'll see what I mean.

During the 2020 onset of the coronavirus pandemic, many learned to cut costs. For some, that amounted to skipping their decadent latte. For others, however, cutbacks became acute. According to data compiled by Age Wave and Edward Jones, 32 percent of Americans plan to retire later than planned because of the pandemic. Women felt a more adverse effect. The report stipulated that 41 percent of women continued to save for retirement, compared to 58 percent of men.[57]

---

[57] Megan Leonhardt. cnbc.com. June 16, 2021. "58% of men were able to continue saving for retirement during the pandemic—but only 41% of women were." https://www.cnbc.com/2021/06/16/why-pandemic-hit-womens-retirement-savings-more-than-mens.html

More Health Care Needs

In addition to the cost of living for a longer lifespan is the fact aging, plain and simple, means more health care, and more health care means more money. Women are survivors. They suffer from the morbidity-mortality paradox, which states women suffer more non-fatal illnesses throughout their lifetime than men, who experience fewer illnesses but higher mortality.

Women have been found to seek treatment more often when not feeling well and emphasize staying healthy when older, according to studies. Survival, I believe, is on the side of the woman. However, surviving things, like cancer, also means more checkups later in life.

A statistical concern for women involves the prospect of long-term care. Long-term care for women lasts 3.7 years on average compared to 2.2 years for men.[58]

Widowhood

Not only do women typically live longer than their same-age male counterparts, they also stand a greater chance of living alone as they age. Some divorce, separate or never marry. Among those age sixty-five and over, 33 percent of women live alone compared to 20 percent of men.[59]

I don't write this to scare people; rather, I think it's fundamentally important to prepare my female clients for something that may be a startling, *but very likely,* scenario. At some point, most women will have to handle their financial situations on their own. A little preparation can go a long way,

---

[58] Lindsay Modglin. singlecare.com. February 15, 2022. "Long-term care statistics 2022" https://www.singlecare.com/blog/news/long-term-care-statistics/

[59] statistica.com. November 23, 2022. "Share of senior households living alone in the United States 2020, by gender" https://www.statista.com/statistics/912400/senior-households-living-alone-usa/

and having a basic understanding of your household finances and the "who, what, where, and how much" of your family's assets is incredibly useful—it can prevent a tragic situation from being more traumatic.

In my opinion, the financial services industry sometimes underserves women in these situations. Some financial professionals tend to alienate women, even when their spouses are alive. I've heard several stories of women who sat through meeting after meeting without their financial professional ever addressing a single question to them.

In our firm, when we work with couples, we work hard to make sure our retirement income strategies work for *both* people. No matter who is the financial alpha, it's important for everyone who is affected by a retirement strategy to understand it.

Our firm takes a very gentle approach to help widows by trying to be proactive during the planning process. We believe that during the grieving process, one of the last things you should do is make lifelong financial decisions. One of the things we do is help women gather and recognize all of their assets, so they understand their income streams. Second, we help them determine how much income they will need after their spouses passes away. Third, we determine how many assets they have. And fourth, we examine whether legal instruments are in place to assure that their assets will transfer to their beneficiaries.

I find it tremendously rewarding to sit down with people in the deepest parts of their grieving process and help them think logically. We gather all the information we need and put together a plan for them that strives to provide peace.

Taxes

One of the often-unexpected aspects of widowhood is the tax bill. Many women continue similar lifestyles to the ones they shared with their spouses. This, in turn, means continuing to have a similar need for income. However, after the death of a spouse, their taxes will be calculated based on a single filer's income table, which is much less forgiving than the couple's tax rates. With proper planning, your financial professional and tax advisor may be able to help you take the sting out of your new tax status.

Caregiving

Of the 53 million caregivers providing unpaid, informal care for older adults in 2020, 61 percent are women. Among today's family caregivers, 61 percent work and 45 percent report some kind of financial impact from providing a loved one care and support.[60] In addition to the financial burden created by caregiving responsibilities, women devote an average of 5.7 hours each day to duties such as housekeeping and looking after loved ones. [61] So then, when can women find the time to focus long and hard on financial matters?

Unfortunately, the impact and hardships created by traditional roles for women typically do not account for Social Security benefit losses or the losses of health care benefits and retirement savings. This also doesn't account for maternity care, mothers who homeschool, or women who leave the workforce to care for their children in any way.

I don't repeat these statistics to scare you. Estimates typically place the monetary value of unofficial caregiving services across the United States at around $150 billion or more. Yet, I think the emotional value of the care many women provide their elderly relatives or neighbors cannot be quantified. So, to be clear, this shouldn't be taken as a "why not to provide caregiving" spiel. Instead, it should be seen as a call for "why to *prepare* for caregiving" or "how to lessen the financial and emotional burden of caregiving."

[60] caregiving.org. 2020 Report. "Caregiving in the U.S. 2020."
https://www.caregiving.org/caregiving-in-the-us-2020/
[61] Drew Weisholtz. Today. January 22, 2020. "Women do 2 more hours of housework daily than men, study says."
https://www.today.com/news/women-do-2-more-hours-housework-daily-men-study-says-t172272

Funding Your Own Retirement

For these reasons, women need to be prepared to fund more of their own retirements. There are several savings options and products, including the spousal 401(k). Unlike a traditional 401(k), where you contribute money to a plan with your employer, a spousal 401(k) is something your spouse sets up on your behalf, so he or she can contribute a portion of the paycheck to your retirement funds. This is something to consider, particularly for families where one spouse has dropped out of the workforce to care for a relative.

Also, if you find yourself in a caregiving role, talk to your employer's human resources department. Some companies have paid leave, special circumstance, or sick leave options you could qualify for, making it easier to cope and helping you stay in the workforce longer.

Saving Money

Women need more money to fund their retirements, period. But this doesn't have to be a significant burden—often, women are better at saving, while usually taking less risk in their portfolios.[62] This gives me reason to believe, as women get more involved in their finances, families will continue to be better-prepared for retirement, both *his* and *hers*.

---

[62] Maurie Backman. The Motley Fool. March 4, 2021. "A Summary of 20 Years of Research and Statistics on Women in Investing." https://www.fool.com/research/women-in-investing-research/

CHAPTER 10
Charity

Wills and testaments, trusts and powers of attorney—these are all pieces of what we often call legacy planning. But I would be remiss if I didn't address a piece of legacy preparation near and dear to my heart: charitable contributions.

Charity is one of those universal concepts that unites us as human beings. Football players who dedicate their resources to building homes for single moms, communities who help neighbors rebuild after catastrophes, groundskeepers who donate millions from under a mattress to their favorite university, or private donors who put impoverished children through school. . .these are the stories that inspire us, that drive us to be better people.

There are many, many ways to pass money to your favorite charity, university, foundation, or public resource. Some include using qualified charitable distributions with the mandatory withdrawals from your IRA, and others lend themselves to establishing trusts. Whatever your preferred method of charitable distribution, the right financial professional will partner with a qualified tax advisor and/or estate planning attorney to discover how to help you make your contributions in a way that fits well within your own strategy for taxes—helping to ensure your contributions are passed efficiently to your intended beneficiary.

Many of our clients are charitable-minded. They love to give to charity, whether it be something in ministry, or something related to animals, or something regarding the environment. Many people have many different interests.

One of our greatest blessings is to show them how they can give to those organizations in a tax-efficient and sometimes tax-free way. These strategies can help increase the impact of the dollars that they give.

We implement strategies that center on qualified charitable distributions and charitable donations. We also look into the possibility of giving donor-advised funds. All of these tools were enacted by the United States government to allow you to give to charitable organizations and do so in a way that can be advantageous to your tax obligations.

We have seen many charities benefit tremendously, and we have seen many clients whose hearts have swollen with pride, by watching their dollars go to use for causes that are dear to them.

Where to Start?

We've all heard it is better to give than to receive, and science backs this up. Multiple studies show those who give to charity or volunteer experience less depression, lower blood pressure, higher self-esteem, and greater happiness.[63]

It's a common perception, however, that retirees are less inclined to be charitable. It seems like reasoned logic—they're living on fixed incomes, and it's difficult to work charitable giving into conservative strategies designed to protect assets. But this counters the facts. In 2021, more baby boomers donated to charities than any other generations.[64]

---

[63] "Volunteering and Its Surprising Benefits." https://www.helpguide.org/articles/healthy-living/volunteering-and-its-surprising-benefits.htm
[64] Dawn Papandrea. lendingtree.com. November 29, 2021. "56% of Americans Donated to Charity in 2021, at Average of $574." https://www.lendingtree.com/debt-consolidation/charitable-donations-survey-study/

So, how do we keep up—or even increase—our donations in retirement? Well, as with all the other topics we cover in this book, step one is to build charitable giving into our retirement plans. Advanced planning can help you be sure your donations—at least in the monetary sense—are given in the most tax-efficient and effective way, both for you and for the charity to which you are contributing.

Planned Giving: Lifetime

When we reference charitable contributions, it's important to distinguish between lifetime giving and charitable giving as part of a well-prepared estate plan.

The American tax system has many provisions to encourage charitable giving. I'm sure the reasoning goes something along the lines of, if we the people were naturally able, through our own means, to care for the poor and vulnerable in our own communities, we collectively would need to pay fewer taxes to support federal aid to those same people. It's a wonderful consideration, and one we should all aspire to. But, in practice, it gets more difficult, as tax codes change and shift according to political administrations and other public considerations. Ensuring your charitable contributions are tax-efficient is not a one-time move—it requires yearly analysis.

It's important to remember your charitable giving is most effective when the combined amount of your *itemized* deductions is more than your *standard* deduction. Now it isn't only charity that counts toward your itemized deduction; there are also homeowner and business owner credits, adoption credits, etc. But, as it pertains to charity, if you haven't contributed a significant amount to charity in a certain tax year, it may not be worth counting on your taxes.

Deductions change year-to-year, of course, but the IRS usually publishes the following year's charts in November. When you're itemizing deductions, you may deduct up to 50 percent of your adjusted gross (pre-tax) income, though in some cases, 20 percent and 30 percent limitations apply.[65]

Another thing to keep in mind if you are considering the tax implications of a charitable donation, you must have a receipt, a canceled check, or some demonstrable way of recording the transaction. Additionally, many charitable activities aren't eligible for tax credits. Raffle tickets, charity event entrance fees, and those sorts of things are not typically counted as charitable deductions on your taxes—a quick rule of thumb is, if you received something in return for your donation, it's not tax-deductible.

Perhaps one of the most crucial things to keep in mind when it comes to the tax implications of charitable giving, however, is "nonprofit" doesn't mean "tax-advantaged." The IRS keeps a long list of organizations that qualify for tax-deducted gifting in the Internal Revenue Code section 501(c)(3). Yet, many excellent nonprofits and civic organizations are not 501(c)(3)s. That doesn't mean you shouldn't give to them—truly, charity is *not* about tax deductions when it comes right down to it—it just means you shouldn't plan to include it as part of your tax-efficiency strategies.

Again, I would be remiss to not emphasize that these laws and definitions change year to year, so it is important to work with a team of qualified financial and tax professionals who can help you plan for the future and adjust to the times, in addition to verifying whether the charity you are considering is tax-exempt.

While impermanence seems to be a fixture of our tax system, one important aspect of charity tax law was made permanent for the foreseeable future. In 2015, Congress passed a budget deal signed into law by President Barack Obama. Among the provisions of the "Protecting Americans From Tax Hikes Act of 2015," which included this important measure:

---

[65] IRS.gov. August 25, 2022. "Charitable Contribution Deductions" https://www.irs.gov/charities-non-profits/charitable-organizations/charitable-contribution-deductions#.

IRA charitable rollovers — at age seventy-and-one-half, owners of traditional IRAs can make direct gifts of up to $100,000 a year to a qualified charity directly from the IRA.[66] This is known as a qualified charitable distribution, or QCD.

What makes permanent deduction No. 3 so important is a person who uses an IRA to contribute to charity in this way can: 1. Be charitable, 2. Avoid having their RMDs push them into a higher tax bracket by instead gifting them to those in need, 3. Take advantage of the tax-free aspect of a QCD when planning charitable gifting, and 4. Potentially use the tax break to offset other tax consequences, like the tax on appreciated assets or capital gains. Please note, though, since the SECURE Act allows IRA contributions after an individual reaches age seventy-three, QCDs will be adversely affected (not all of the listed benefits will still apply) if a contribution is made to that IRA in the same year a QCD is withdrawn.[67]

When a person reaches the age where they must begin paying taxes on required minimum distributions (seventy-three), they can then employ something called a qualified charitable distribution. That simply means you can take money from an IRA or a 401(k) and you can distribute it to the charity of your choice. You can do so in a tax-free manner.

We bring these ideas to our clients every year during the account review process and ask them if they still have the desire to give charitably. If so, we help instruct them on which bucket of money might be best to use for a donation. We examine the potential tax consequences, often in concert with their tax advisor, and how a qualified charitable distribution can fit their situation.

---

[66] Council on Foundations. 2022. "IRA Charitable Rollover" https://www.cof.org/content/ira-charitable-rollover-0#:~:text=As%20of%20December%2018%2C%202015,recognize%20the%20distribution%20as%20income.

[67] Bob Carlson. Forbes. January 28,2020. "More Questions and Answers About the SECURE Act." https://www.forbes.com/sites/bobcarlson/2020/01/28/more-questions-and-answers-about-the-secure-act/#113d49564869

Planned Giving: After My Lifetime

For many charities, endowments and legacy gifts are the lifeblood that keeps them going. And, for many of us, a large final gift is an excellent way to continue a legacy of giving into perpetuity. The financial reasons for final charitable gifts, much like the annual contributions we often give, are many and, mostly, tax-based. A large final gift can be a good way to offload highly appreciated assets, allowing our favorite charities to experience the full use of an asset without us having to pay out a sizable tax bill.

Many charities have gone to great lengths to make this an attractive option, with some having preferences for certain donation types and strategies. For instance, many public entities, such as libraries and schools, have foundations to collect most of the donations and do major fundraising. Churches and universities often have special projects and intentional funding that stems from sizable endowments.

There are many financial vehicles to help you meet your charitable goals and give you benefits during your lifetime as well—from permanent life insurance policies to charitable trusts and charitable annuities. That's why it's important to plan ahead and work with a goal in mind. If you have some idea of what end you want to achieve, it can be easier to find the estate attorneys, tax professionals, and financial professionals who will be best qualified to help.

Non-Monetary Charitable Contributions

Ultimately, aside from the tax breaks, the good feeling, and the name on a park bench you might receive, your charitable contributions aren't about what you "get" in return. This is one other reason we should plan ahead for our good works; it's about doing the right thing.

Volunteering is one great, non-monetary way to support the charities and causes we believe in. Like I noted earlier, research shows retirees who are active and engaged volunteers in their communities often have a better sense of purpose and report more happiness than those who aren't. In volunteering, we have a reason to get up in the morning, and we meet new people and make friends. These are all things that may previously have stemmed from your nine-to-five workday but tend to fall by the wayside after leaving the workforce, making this consideration even more important.

Every year in our firm, we partner with a charitable organization and include our clients in this process. We have allowed our clients to choose which charitable organization we would assist and then offer clients work days or volunteer days where we go as a group and do things for our local community.

The tremendous heartfelt impact is amazing to see unfold. We have packaged food for the less fortunate, provided personal hygiene items for those who cannot afford them, and helped the homeless in our local community shelters. To watch our clients be part of this by volunteering their time has overwhelmed me and warmed my heart. We believe that our community is where we have been planted, and that is where we are to grow. I believe whatever we can do to benefit those around us who are less fortunate enables us to all take a step above in this world.

CHAPTER 11

Finding a Financial Professional

The reason that I joined the financial services industry is because I grew up in a home where financial intelligence was seemingly minimal. I watched my parents struggle for years and years trying to raise five children. It just seemed like there had to be a better way.

It seemed like my friends and their families knew something that we didn't. The information I lacked drove me to try and understand things better. Through that drive for knowledge, I realized that many more people like me needed help. Among those people, we could help steer them in a better direction. I realized that the outcome could significantly improve by doing a little bit of planning. Then I realized that dreams are actually something that can come true, but it takes planning, it takes education, it takes diligence, and it takes commitment. I realized if I could be the person who could help somebody better their life, then, yes, that's what I wanted to do.

All of the advisors in our firm, including me, also possess life insurance licenses. Our education is ongoing. We attend conferences, and we have continuing education that must be completed on an annual basis. We believe an educated advisor can be a great advisor, but we also believe that an advisor needs to be on the same side of the table as the client. What I mean by that is the advisor's advice needs to benefit the client and not the advisor or the advisor's firm.

That's not to say we are not going to be paid for our services, but our goal is to help you reach your retirement goals. We are an independent financial services firm, and we strive to offer our clients a high level of customer service and build relationships with our clients to help them pursue their goals in retirement.

One of the biggest reasons I believe people should not do their financial planning all by themselves is because emotion can influence decisions. If you employ a professional, then logic can take over because that professional has no emotional ties to your money. They have no emotional ties to markets moving up and down. They can simply apply logical plans that have tested themselves over time, and the outcome can be better because you have removed human emotion.

Today, retirement looks much different than it did thirty years ago, perhaps even ten years ago, simply because people are retiring earlier and living longer. Things like pension plans and Social Security plans have changed drastically and, in some cases, gone away completely. We believe now that it is crucial that you take control of your financial future and you know where you're going as far as forty years down the road. Longevity is not something that we believe should be taken lightly. We believe you could have a tremendous retirement with a bit of planning.

We believe you should look for a financial professional who will put together a complete financial plan and not just recommend financial products.

A red flag should be someone who recommends a mutual fund, an annuity, a stock or a bond, or some other form of financial instrument, without asking enough questions and building a financial plan that fits your income and legacy needs while accounting for taxes.

There are many ways a financial professional can be compensated. They can charge a planning fee, they can charge a commission, they can charge a management fee, or they can charge a consulting fee. Make sure you know the answer to the question about how a financial professional is being compensated before you decide to work with an advisor and the company they represent.

Our primary goal in our firm as it pertains to our clients is to make sure they have a financial plan that will weather the storms of time. We will see ups and downs in the market. We will experience life and death. Good and bad times will transpire. A financial retirement plan that weathers diverse economic situations and accounts for various factors and considerations is best. Whether interest rates rise, stock markets fall, inflation goes up, or Social Security goes down, you need a plan that weathers all of the what-ifs of what could come in the future. Then you can also plan for a fulfilling retirement.

I want to take you back to the story I shared in the preface. Dad, we have a problem! Those are the words that I heard on the other end of the phone at 2 o'clock in the morning. My eighteen-year-old daughter had been driving her car when a tire came off. She made a call no parent wants to field in the middle of the night and began telling me of the mishap.

As any dad would do, I jumped out of bed and drove as fast as I could to where she got stranded. My mind raced uncontrollably, knowing she pulled over on the side of the road and needed to ensure she was okay.

Thankfully, I found her and drove her home safe and sound.

Just that morning, I had new tires put on her car. The technician failed to tighten the lug nuts, and the tire literally came off the car. This could have turned out much worse than it did. Thankfully, the outcome is nothing more than a funny story told by a father who still thinks about the disastrous way his daughter's car breakdown could have gone.

So what is my point? Why am I telling you this?

Because just a tiny detail and some attention to excellence would have allowed my daughter to drive safely. Instead, someone did a sloppy job putting new tires on her vehicle and called it good, placing a teenage girl in danger and potentially changing her life.

Fees

In recent years, advertising in your local newspaper has diminished. So too has the size of the paper. More people are accustomed to reading news online, or look for other sources, including those without a paywall. Advertisers don't find as much value in placing ads in the actual print version of the paper. Declines in circulation are to blame. Also, many former advertisers have company websites, which they use to drive consumer traffic.

However, if you happen to be someone who receives the newspaper in your driveway, you might have noticed that grocery store circulars are still a thing. Sure, the circulars might be a bit smaller. Yet, grocers still see some advantages to listing numerous prices for sales items in print, which readers can often scan much easier than looking up individual items on a website.

Those newspaper ads continue to be printed as a service to consumers. They want to see prices—in some cases before they ever step into the store—so they can prepare their shopping lists accordingly.

Why then should the cost of doing business with a financial professional often seem like a clandestine mystery? Well, to be blunt, it shouldn't. Consumers should know how much it will cost them to work with a financial professional and how exactly they arrive at the fees charged.

Now, fees can be troublesome. You can't get something for nothing, and fees are how many financial companies and professionals make a living. Yet, it's important to recognize even a fee of a single percentage point is money out of your pocket—money that represents not just the one-time fee of today but also represents an opportunity cost. One study found a single percentage point fee could cost a millennial close to

$600,000 over forty years of saving.[68] For someone approaching retirement, how much do you think fees may have cost them over their lifetime?

It is important to look at management fees and assess if you think you're getting what you pay for. Over the course of ten years, these fees can add up, and you may have decades ahead of you in which you will need to rely on your assets.

---

[68] Dayana Yochim, Jonathan Todd. NerdWallet. "How a 1% Fee Could Cost Millennials $590,000 in Retirement Savings." https://www.nerdwallet.com/blog/investing/millennial-retirement-fees-one-percent-half-million-savings-impact/

About the Author

PHIL COOPER, 210 FINANCIAL

Phil Cooper is the founder and CEO of 210 Financial, a company he launched in 2000. He has spent more than twenty-five years in multiple areas of the financial industry and has been an Investment Adviser Representative for eighteen years. He serves his clients as an Investment Adviser Representative and licensed insurance agent.

Phil passed both the Series 63 and 65 securities exams and holds a bachelor's degree in biblical studies and an associate degree in electronic engineering.

A strong passion for Bible prophecy prompted Phil to travel to Israel with his wife of over 25 years, Kelly. Phil's favorite book is the Bible. In his spare time, he enjoys riding ATVs or watching the St. Louis Cardinals.

Phil and Kelly have three children, Carrie, Katie and Mac; a son-in-law, Kendall; and grandsons, Kyser and Cashton.

Working at 210 Financial enables Phil to build a legacy with his children and treat clients like extended family. Phil's passion is building financial retirement plans that inspire confidence.

Morton, Illinois
100 B. Yordy Road
Morton, Illinois 61550
Phone: 309.263.1333

Bloomington, Illinois
3801 GE Road, Suite 2A
Bloomington, Illinois 61704

Davenport, Iowa
100 Kimberly Rd. Suite 704
Davenport, Iowa 52806
Phone: 563.253.7993

Email: office@210Financial.com
Web: 210financial.com

Made in the USA
Monee, IL
07 February 2023

27229831R00079